CITIZENS

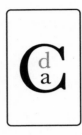

Published in association with the Centre for Canadian Studies at Mount Allison University. Information on the Canadian Democratic Audit project can be found at www.CanadianDemocraticAudit.ca.

Advisory Group

William Cross, Director (Mount Allison University)
R. Kenneth Carty (University of British Columbia)
Elisabeth Gidengil (McGill University)
Richard Sigurdson (University of New Brunswick)
Frank Strain (Mount Allison University)
Michael Tucker (Mount Allison University)

Titles

John Courtney, *Elections*
William Cross, *Political Parties*
Elisabeth Gidengil, André Blais, Neil Nevitte, and Richard Nadeau, *Citizens*
David Docherty, *Legislatures*
Jennifer Smith, *Federalism*
Lisa Young and Joanna Everitt, *Advocacy Groups*
Darin Barney, *Communications Technology*
Ian Greene, *The Courts*
Graham White, *Cabinets and First Ministers*

CITIZENS

Elisabeth Gidengil,
André Blais,
Neil Nevitte,
Richard Nadeau

UBCPress

© UBC Press 2004

15 14 13 12 11 10 09 08 07 06 05 04   5 4 3 2 1

Printed in Canada on acid-free paper that is 100% post-consumer recycled, processed chlorine-free, and printed with vegetable-based, low-VOC inks.

National Library of Canada Cataloguing in Publication

Citizens / Elisabeth Gidengil ... [et al.].

(Canadian democratic audit ; 3)
Includes bibliographical references and index.
ISBN 0-7748-1101-3 (set). – ISBN 0-7748-0919-1

1. Political participation – Canada. 2. Citizenship – Canada. 3. Democracy – Canada.
I. Gidengil, Elisabeth, 1947- II. Series.

JL187.C55 2004   323'.042'0971   C2004-902511-2

Canadä

UBC Press gratefully acknowledges the financial support for our publishing program of the Government of Canada through the Book Publishing Industry Development Program (BPIDP), and of the Canada Council for the Arts, and the British Columbia Arts Council.

The Centre for Canadian Studies thanks the Harold Crabtree Foundation for its support of the Canadian Democratic Audit project. Much of the research on which this volume is based was funded by the Social Sciences and Humanities Research Council of Canada. The authors also gratefully acknowledge the financial support of Elections Canada, the Institute for Research on Public Policy, and their respective universities.

Copy editor: Sarah Wight
Text design: Peter Ross, Counterpunch
Typesetter: Artegraphica Design Co. Ltd.
Proofreader: Rob Giannetto
Indexer: Noeline Bridge

UBC Press
The University of British Columbia
2029 West Mall
Vancouver, BC V6T 1Z2
604-822-5959 / Fax: 604-822-6083
www.ubcpress.ca

Contents

Figures

FOREWORD

This volume is part of the Canadian Democratic Audit series. The objective of this series is to consider how well Canadian democracy is performing at the outset of the twenty-first century. In recent years, political and opinion leaders, government commissions, academics, citizen groups, and the popular press have all identified a "democratic deficit" and "democratic malaise" in Canada. These characterizations often are portrayed as the result of a substantial decline in Canadians' confidence in their democratic practices and institutions. Indeed, Canadians are voting in record low numbers, many are turning away from the traditional political institutions, and a large number are expressing declining confidence in both their elected politicians and the electoral process.

Nonetheless, Canadian democracy continues to be the envy of much of the rest of the world. Living in a relatively wealthy and peaceful society, Canadians hold regular elections in which millions cast ballots. These elections are largely fair, efficient, and orderly events. They routinely result in the selection of a government with no question about its legitimate right to govern. Developing democracies from around the globe continue to look to Canadian experts for guidance in establishing electoral practices and democratic institutions. Without a doubt, Canada is widely seen as a leading example of successful democratic practice.

Given these apparently competing views, the time is right for a comprehensive examination of the state of Canadian democracy. Our purposes are to conduct a systematic review of the operations of Canadian democracy, to listen to what others have to say about Canadian democracy, to assess its strengths and weaknesses, to consider where there are opportunities for advancement, and to evaluate popular reform proposals.

A democratic audit requires the setting of benchmarks for evaluation of the practices and institutions to be considered. This necessarily involves substantial consideration of the meaning of democracy.

"Democracy" is a contested term and we are not interested here in striking a definitive definition. Nor are we interested in a theoretical model applicable to all parts of the world. Rather we are interested in identifying democratic benchmarks relevant to Canada in the twenty-first century. In selecting these we were guided by the issues raised in the current literature on Canadian democratic practice and by the concerns commonly raised by opinion leaders and found in public opinion data. We have settled on three benchmarks: public participation, inclusiveness, and responsiveness. We believe that any contemporary definition of Canadian democracy must include institutions and decision-making practices that are defined by public participation, that this participation include all Canadians, and that government outcomes respond to the views of Canadians.

While settling on these guiding principles, we have not imposed a strict set of democratic criteria on all of the evaluations that together constitute the Audit. Rather, our approach allows the auditors wide latitude in their evaluations. While all auditors keep the benchmarks of participation, inclusiveness, and responsiveness central to their examinations, each adds additional criteria of particular importance to the subject he or she is considering. We believe this approach of identifying unifying themes, while allowing for divergent perspectives, enhances the project by capturing the robustness of the debate surrounding democratic norms and practices.

We decided at the outset to cover substantial ground and to do so in a relatively short period. These two considerations, coupled with a desire to respond to the most commonly raised criticisms of the contemporary practice of Canadian democracy, result in a series that focuses on public institutions, electoral practices, and new phenomena that are likely to affect democratic life significantly. The series includes volumes that examine key public decision-making bodies: legislatures, the courts, and cabinets and government. The structures of our democratic system are considered in volumes devoted to questions of federalism and the electoral system. The ways in which citizens participate in electoral politics and policy making are a crucial component of the project, and thus we include studies of interest groups and political parties. The desire and capacity of Canadians for meaningful participation in public life is also the subject of a volume. Finally, the challenges and opportunities raised by new communication technologies are also considered. The Audit does not include studies devoted to the status of particular groups of Canadians. Rather than separate out Aboriginals, women, new Canadians, and others, these groups are treated together with all Canadians throughout the Audit.

In all, this series includes nine volumes examining specific areas of Canadian democratic life. A tenth, synthetic volume provides an overall assessment and makes sense out of the different approaches and findings found in the rest of the series. Our examination is not exhaustive. Canadian democracy is a vibrant force, the status of which can never be fully captured at one time. Nonetheless the areas we consider involve many of the pressing issues currently facing democracy in Canada. We do not expect to have the final word on this subject. Rather, we hope to encourage others to pursue similar avenues of inquiry.

A project of this scope cannot be accomplished without the support of many individuals. At the top of the list of those deserving credit are the members of the Canadian Democratic Audit team. From the very beginning, the Audit has been a team effort. This outstanding group of academics has spent many hours together, defining the scope of the project, prodding each other on questions of Canadian democracy, and most importantly, supporting one another throughout the endeavour, all with good humour. To Darin Barney, André Blais, Kenneth Carty, John Courtney, David Docherty, Joanna Everitt, Elisabeth Gidengil, Ian Greene, Richard Nadeau, Neil Nevitte, Richard Sigurdson, Jennifer Smith, Frank Strain, Michael Tucker, Graham White, and Lisa Young I am forever grateful.

The Centre for Canadian Studies at Mount Allison University has been my intellectual home for several years. The Centre, along with the Harold Crabtree Foundation, has provided the necessary funding and other assistance necessary to see this project through to fruition. At Mount Allison University, Peter Ennals provided important support to this project when others were skeptical; Wayne MacKay and Michael

Fox have continued this support since their respective arrivals on campus; and Joanne Goodrich and Peter Loewen have provided important technical and administrative help.

The University of British Columbia Press, particularly its senior acquisitions editor, Emily Andrew, has been a partner in this project from the very beginning. Emily has been involved in every important decision and has done much to improve the result. Camilla Jenkins has overseen the copyediting and production process and in doing so has made these books better. Scores of Canadian and international political scientists have participated in the project as commentators at our public conferences, as critics at our private meetings, as providers of quiet advice, and as referees of the volumes. The list is too long to name them all, but David Cameron, Sid Noel, Leslie Seidle, Jim Bickerton, Alexandra Dobrowolsky, Livianna Tossutti, Janice Gross Stein, and Frances Abele all deserve special recognition for their contributions. We are also grateful to the Canadian Study of Parliament Group, which partnered with us for our inaugural conference in Ottawa in November 2001.

Finally, this series is dedicated to all of the men and women who contribute to the practice of Canadian democracy. Whether as active participants in parties, groups, courts, or legislatures, or in the media and the universities, without them Canadian democracy would not survive.

William Cross
Director, The Canadian Democratic Audit
Sackville, New Brunswick

CITIZENS

AUDITING DEMOCRATIC CITIZENSHIP 1

Citizens are at the core of any meaningful definition of democracy. For this reason alone, they must be included in an audit of Canadian democracy. In the pages that follow we ask two key questions about democratic citizenship in Canada: how engaged are Canadians in the country's democratic life, and which Canadians are most – and least – engaged? The answers to these questions bear very directly on the benchmarks of responsiveness, inclusiveness, and participation that define the Canadian Democratic Audit project. These three benchmarks are indissolubly linked. Knowing who participates in public life and, more significantly, who does not, provides critical insights into the inclusiveness of Canadian democracy. And knowing who is included in Canada's democratic life and who is left out tells us, in turn, whose needs and wants are most likely to be addressed by government and whose may get ignored.

Equally important, an audit of democratic citizenship can illuminate the performance of our democratic institutions. Fewer Canadians than ever are exercising their right to vote. If citizens are uninterested and uninvolved in democratic politics, it is tempting to blame the citizens themselves. However, we should be prompted to ask *why* these citizens are apathetic about politics. Do the political parties fail to provide meaningful choices? Do the media fail to convey the parties' messages to the voters? Do the political parties and the media contribute to a climate of cynicism and disaffection with politics? Or does the problem lie with "representative institutions" that systematically underrepresent some segments of the population? Providing a comprehensive answer to these questions is beyond the scope of this audit, but raising them underlines the fact that an audit of democratic citizenship must be seen as an integral component of the larger project of auditing Canadian democracy.

Finally, an audit of democratic citizenship can cast light on the deeper roots of democratic malaise. Canadian society is marked by disparities in income and education and by differences in the power and status of groups like women and racial minorities. We cannot overlook the potential impact of these structural inequalities on the level and nature of citizens' political engagement. We have to ask whether structural inequalities create democratic divides. In other words, are some citizens less engaged than others because they have fewer resources at their disposal?

Assessing Democratic Divides

In order to explore the possible links between structural inequalities and political (dis)engagement, we focus on five dimensions: age, education, income, sex, and race. Throughout the text, we make comparisons across generations and educational levels, between rich and poor and men and women, and between members of visible minorities and Canadians at large. The goal is to determine whether there are systematic differences in the level and nature of political engagement across these societal divides.

Ronald Inglehart (1971; 1990) has been a particularly forceful proponent of the view that generation matters. He has highlighted the differences in the formative experiences of those born since the end of the Second World War and those born earlier. According to Inglehart, this generational divide has been characterized by a shift from materialist to postmaterialist values. The postwar generations have enjoyed a period of relative peace and unprecedented prosperity. Where their parents and grandparents had to contend with the privations of the Depression and world war, many of those born since 1945 have been able to take their economic and physical security more or less for granted. As material needs have been satisfied, needs for self-actualization have taken on a new importance. Along with this cultural shift has come structural change. Canada's transformation from an industrial to a postindustrial society has been accompanied by greatly expanded access to higher education, the emergence of a new middle class of managers, professionals, and technocrats, and the increasingly rapid spread of new information and communications technologies. As a result more citizens than ever before have ready access to information, along with the cognitive skills and the motivation to put that information to work for them (Dalton 1984).

Taken together, cognitive mobilization and the rise of postmaterialist values have potentially far-reaching implications for democratic citizenship (Nevitte 1996). Postmaterialist values fuel a desire for more autonomous forms of political engagement; cognitive mobilization allows that desire to be realized. Citizens who share these attributes are likely to want more meaningful forms of political involvement than the traditional, hierarchically organized institutions of democratic governance typically allow. This raises a critical question: are these citizens abandoning the traditional vehicles of political participation, like political parties and interest groups, in favour of community involvement and more unconventional modes of political action, or are they simply broadening their repertoire of political activities?

In order to pursue these questions, we distinguish four generations: the pre-baby boomers (born before 1945), the baby boomers (born between 1945 and 1959), generation X (born between 1960 and 1969), and post-generation X (born since 1970). The baby boomers are the postmaterialist generation par excellence. These are the Canadians who have been the major beneficiaries of the long period of peace and prosperity that followed the end of the Second World War. Circumstances have not been so propitious for those born since 1960. They have had to contend with recession and with the restructuring that accompanied the spread of globalization. And it is not just the economic times that have changed. When they were beginning to reach adulthood, disaffection with politics was growing. This disaffection reflected a combination of factors: the rise of a neoconservative ideology that advocated a smaller role for the state, a perception that national governments were relatively powerless in the face of global economic forces, and a series of constitutional crises and failed accords. According to some popular commentary, these circumstances have produced a disengaged generation that often tunes out politics altogether.

The term "generation X" is taken from Douglas Coupland's (1991) book of the same name. Some apply the label to anyone born since 1960, but it is more revealing to distinguish between those who had already reached adulthood when *Generation X* was published and those who came later. The latter may also be turning their backs on electoral politics, but there is an optimistic belief that they are turning to other, more meaningful forms of political engagement instead. Media images have shown young people protesting against globalization at a series of meetings of world leaders: the Asia-Pacific Economic Cooperation meeting in Vancouver in 1997, the World Trade Organization Summit in Seattle in 2000, and the Summit of the Americas in Quebec City in 2001. But we need to ask just how representative these images are and whether young Canadians are indeed embracing protest activities in greater numbers than their parents or grandparents. In order to do so, we treat post-generation X Canadians, those born since 1970, as a separate group.

One factor that could be expected to counteract disengagement is education. Education seems to be good for democracy, because it helps people to understand how democracy works (Dewey 1916). The democratic process is inherently messy, necessitating complex compromises that take time and effort to achieve. This can cause frustration – and withdrawal from democratic politics – on the part of those who do not appreciate what is entailed (Hibbing and Theiss-Morse 1995). Education not only makes people more sophisticated about politics but also makes them more open-minded and tolerant of opposing viewpoints

(Stouffer 1955; Selznick and Steinberg 1969; Hyman and Wright 1979). In addition, education seems to foster civic spirit and norms of civic engagement. These are important because they can motivate people to participate even when they might otherwise be disinclined.

Education also equips people with the cognitive skills that are required for meaningful participation. Reading about politics in the newspaper or going on-line to access political information on the Internet requires basic literacy, as does marking a ballot paper or signing a petition. Political participation also presumes an ability to deal with complexity. Citizens are bombarded with a mass of information on issues that may seem remote from their day-to-day concerns. Not only do they have to sift through this information, they have to try to "read between the lines" and to separate fact from rhetoric. Education helps people to meet this challenge. Finally, education is associated with social networks in which politics is likely to be a topic of conversation. This gives people an incentive to pay attention to politics so that they can join in the discussion, and these discussions, in turn, can be a source of new information about politics.

If this is all so, we have a puzzle: unprecedented numbers of Canadians are graduating from university, and yet turnout to vote has declined precipitously since the 1988 federal election. Could it be that the link between education and political engagement is weakening? In order to explore this question, we focus on four educational groups: those who have not completed high school; high school graduates; those who have some postsecondary education; and university graduates.

Lack of education is one reason why poor Canadians might be less politically engaged than their affluent counterparts. But political engagement also requires time, energy, and money. The daily struggle to put food on the table, to pay the bills, and to find money for the rent may sap any desire to follow politics closely. This is especially likely if the daily struggle feeds a perception that the system is not very responsive to the needs and wants of the poor. And even if the will is there, there may not be the money to pay for a babysitter or to travel to party meetings or even to the polls. As for subscribing to a daily newspaper or accessing political information on the Internet, these are luxuries that the poor can ill afford. In order to see just how much difference household income makes to people's level of political engagement, we divide the population into quintiles. This enables us to compare people with household incomes in the bottom 20 percent with those in the middle 20 percent and those in the top 20 percent.

The average Canadian woman continues to have less education and a lower income than the average Canadian man, so we might expect gender differences in political engagement on those grounds alone. However, there are reasons to expect gender differences even when women and men have the same educational qualifications and comparable incomes. Politics remains very much a man's world in Canada. As late as 1980, only 5 percent of MPs in Ottawa were women (see Docherty 2004). That meant just fourteen women. The numbers began to increase in 1984, but in 2000 only 20 percent of those elected to the House of Commons were women. This figure was unchanged from 1997, suggesting that the growth in the number of women MPs may have stalled. The numerical underrepresentation of women in the House of Commons means that women simply do not see themselves when they watch the news or read the newspaper. Only one woman – Kim Campbell – has succeeded in becoming prime minister, and her tenure was brief. Like her New Democrat counterparts, Audrey McLaughlin and Alexa McDonough, Campbell may have been a sacrificial lamb, chosen to lead a party that was doomed to defeat.

Not just the lack of women in politics but the norms that govern political behaviour and media coverage reinforce the notion that politics is a predominantly masculine activity. The news remains very much a "masculine narrative" (Rakow and Kranich 1991, 8). Political coverage is dominated by stereotypically masculine images of the battlefield and the boxing ring (Gidengil and Everitt 1999; 2002; 2003). These images subtly convey the message that women do not really belong in politics. One result may be that many women see politics as just another game that is played – and followed – by men.

Women are not the only group that is numerically underrepresented in Canadian politics. The same is true of visible minorities. Only 17 of the 301 MPs elected in the 2000 federal election belonged to visible minorities (Black 2002). This number was down from the 19 elected to the previous Parliament. According to the 2001 census, visible minorities made up 13.4 percent of the population, and yet they accounted for only 5.6 percent of the MPs elected in the previous year's election. Members of visible minorities may see this small number as emblematic of the racial biases that still permeate Canadian society (Gidengil et al. 2004). The question is whether this makes for a reduced level of interest and involvement in politics on the part of members of visible minorities.

In pursuing this question, we have to be mindful of the fact that the proportion of Canadians who are members of visible minorities has increased substantially over the past thirty years as a result of shifting patterns of immigration. Consequently we need to take account of birthplace as well. If members of visible minorities do prove to be less politically engaged than other Canadians, this could simply reflect the fact that they are more likely to have been born outside Canada. Recent arrivals, in particular, must make significant adjustments in settling into a new environment and in orienting themselves to an unfamiliar political system, and this may depress their involvement in politics. Identifying members of visible minorities from survey data is a difficult task since surveys typically ask about ancestry rather than race. We count anyone who is of non-European origin as being a member of a visible minority. The fit is not perfect, but this approach provides a reasonable approximation.

In a highly regionalized country like Canada, the political importance of place cannot be ignored. We take account of place in a number of ways. First, we document differences in political engagement across the provinces (though caution is warranted when considering figures for Prince Edward Island, given the small sample size). Documenting such differences is easy enough; deciphering their meaning is much trickier. For example, if some provinces have lower levels of political engagement than others this could simply reflect the makeup of their population. According to this type of interpretation, we could expect a less engaged populace in the Atlantic provinces or in Saskatchewan because the residents of these provinces tend to have less education and lower incomes than average. On the other hand, "have" provinces, like Alberta and Ontario, could have lower levels of engagement than the "have-not" provinces as a result of their respective political traditions and political cultures.

Second, we examine whether the type of community in which people live makes a difference to their political engagement. Canada has become an increasingly urban society. According to the 1961 census, almost 40 percent of Canadians lived in rural areas; by the time of the 2001 census, that figure had been cut in half. We need to ask how this has affected the country's democratic life. People who live in small communities are more likely to know their neighbours, and these close social contacts could serve to mobilize them to participate in politics (Oliver 2000). If so, rural Canadians may prove to be more engaged than their urban counterparts.

Finally, we take account of the territorial dimension of Canadian politics by comparing, wherever possible, across levels of government. The extent to which we can actually do this is constrained by the lack of survey data and published studies on political engagement at the provincial and municipal levels. Nonetheless, it is important to make use of whatever data are available because cross-level comparisons bear on a question that has long exercised political thinkers, namely, what is the best size for a democratic polity? As Robert Dahl (1967, 960) noted, there is a tension between the need to foster political engagement and the capacity to attain significant collective goals. While the first consideration seems to argue for smaller political units, the second might suggest larger ones. For their part, provincial governments in Canada have traditionally argued for greater powers by claiming that they are closer to the people. Meanwhile, feminist scholars have pointed to municipal politics as a site that may engage greater interest on the part of women than the traditional arenas of federal and provincial politics. The assumption here is that municipal politics deals with issues that are of more immediate relevance to women's daily lives, such as public safety, recreation, street lighting, and sanitary services. Thus we need to ask whether there are significant differences in political engagement at the federal, provincial, territorial, and municipal levels.

Disaggregating Democratic Engagement

Political engagement presupposes political interest. Unless citizens have a modicum of interest in politics, they are unlikely to devote much time and energy to keeping up with public affairs, and still less to taking an active part in the country's democratic life. Accordingly, Chapter 2 assesses how much interest Canadians have in politics and how much attention they pay to what is going on in the news. This chapter also examines where Canadians get most of their information about politics. Do they rely primarily on the media or do they get most of their information from friends and family? And if they depend on the media, is their primary source television, newspapers, or radio?

This chapter also provides some assessment of how the revolution in communication technologies has affected the amount of attention that Canadians pay to politics. The Internet in particular has been heralded as providing citizens with a new avenue for political engagement. Citizens vary, though, in their capacity and in their motivation to take advantage of the new technologies. The result may be a "digital divide" (Norris 2001) that actually widens the gap between the most engaged and the least engaged citizens. We need to determine whether a digital divide is emerging in Canada.

One reason political interest is important is that it motivates people to acquire information about politics. Information is essential for democratic participation: "Political information is to democratic politics what money is to economics; it is the currency of citizenship" (Delli Carpini and Keeter 1996, 8). If citizens are to hold the government accountable and to authorize a direction for the future, they need information that can help them to ascertain what they want from the government, evaluate the performance of the incumbent, and weigh the respective merits of the alternatives. Its relevance is not limited to forming political preferences, engaging in political debate, or casting a vote; it also underpins such democratic virtues as toleration and mutual respect. Moreover, information seems to soften people's judgments of those who govern, and thereby fosters political trust (Popkin and Dimock 1999). This is because "more knowledgeable citizens tend to judge the behavior of public officials as they judge their own – in the context of circumstances and incentives, with due regard for innocent oversights and errors as well as sheer chance" (Galston 2001, 224).

So Chapter 3 focuses on how much Canadians know about politics. It assesses knowledge of key political actors such as the federal party leaders, the federal finance minister, and provincial premiers, as well as past prime ministers. It also looks at knowledge of party positions. Do Canadians know some of the basic facts that they need to make an informed choice on election day? This chapter also examines how much Canadians learn as a result of election campaigns. In theory, at least, election campaigns provide people who do not pay much attention to politics on a day-to-day basis with the opportunity to acquire information. But do election campaigns really enable the poorly informed to fill in the gaps in their political knowledge? And if they do not, where does the responsibility lie: with citizens who do not care enough to pay attention, or with campaigns that fail to inform?

Some authors have argued that citizens do not need to be well informed: many of them are quite capable of making reasonable political choices even when they do not know the details of the issue at hand. This is because they can make use of information shortcuts (Popkin 1991; Sniderman, Brody, and Tetlock 1991). For example, they may choose to take the same side as a trusted friend who is more knowledgeable. Assuming that the friend shares their interests and values, they will end up making the same choice they would have made if they, too, had taken the trouble to inform themselves. Meanwhile, the "aggregationist" thesis maintains that *collective* public opinion is stable, coherent, and responds predictably to changing conditions, even though many individual expressions of opinion lack those qualities (Page and Shapiro 1992).

Chapter 4 examines whether the use of information shortcuts and aggregation really do compensate for shortfalls in information. Do the poorly informed benefit the most from information shortcuts, or do information shortcuts mainly help the well informed to make better use of their store of knowledge? Would collective opinion really look much as it does now if all Canadians were well informed about politics? This chapter also explores the implications of the uneven distribution of information. Does collective opinion do a better job of reflecting the values and interests of some social groups rather than others? And finally, Chapter 4 asks: what if some Canadians are not simply *un*informed, but *mis*informed? How are policy preferences affected when people get the facts wrong?

Chapter 5 focuses on the benchmark of participation. When we think of participating in politics, we typically think of voting or maybe working on a campaign or joining a political party or interest group. These are all very traditional ways of participating in politics. There are also less conventional modes of participation to consider, such as signing a petition, joining in a boycott, or attending a lawful demonstration. In contrast to the traditional forms of political participation, these activities are not necessarily state centred. Although some may question whether a consumer boycott, say, is truly a political act, it bears on the issue that is at the very core of politics: "who gets what" (Lasswell 1936). Globalization, privatization, and the "shrinking of the state" (Feigenbaum, Henig, and Hamnett 1998) mean that the targets of political engagement now extend well beyond the state to multinational corporations, international agencies, and intergovernmental organizations. Evidence from a range of countries indicates that protest activities are now part of the mainstream (Van Aelst and Walgrave 2001; Norris 2002). Chapter 5 asks whether this is true in Canada, as well.

The steep decline in turnout in federal elections since 1988, examined in Chapter 5, raises an important question: are Canadians turning to other, more meaningful forms of political engagement? Are they abandoning political parties in favour of interest groups? Or are they giving up on traditional vehicles of participation altogether and engaging in various forms of protest politics instead?

Chapter 6 keeps the focus on this question, but looks at participation in civic life more broadly conceived. In doing so, it takes up Robert Putnam's (2000) argument that a healthy democracy requires large stocks of social capital in the form of networks of connection among citizens and norms of trust. The chapter examines involvement in voluntary associations, volunteering, and philanthropy, and asks whether associational activity is indeed related to political engagement.

Establishing Benchmarks and Obtaining Information

Auditing all of these facets of democratic citizenship in Canada cannot take place in a vacuum. We need to have some ways of judging the levels of engagement in civic life. We use two sets of benchmarks wherever possible. First, we compare levels of engagement across time. Are Canadians more or less engaged than they were in years past? Second, we compare levels of engagement in Canada with those in other established Western democracies. Are Canadians more or less engaged than the citizens of comparable countries?

The information comes from a variety of sources. Some is taken from official sources, such as the official election returns filed by the chief electoral officer and by his counterparts in the provinces and the territories. Most of the information comes from surveys, however, including the World Values Surveys, the National Survey on Giving, Volunteering and Participating, and the various surveys archived at the Canadian Opinion Research Archive at Queen's University (CORA).

The chief source of information is the Canadian Election Studies. These studies have been conducted in conjunction with every federal election since 1965, with the exception of the 1972 election. These data offer distinct advantages when it comes to auditing democratic citizenship. Elections are critical moments in a country's democratic life. In an electoral democracy like Canada, they are the basic mechanism through which citizens select the representatives charged with the responsibility of making public policy. In elections, citizens pass judgment on the decisions of the past and authorize a direction for the future. Elections are thus particularly appropriate occasions for assessing the democratic engagement of ordinary Canadians. Equally important, elections permit the evaluation of the performance of the other two key players, the political parties and the media. An election can be likened to a high-speed film that enables us to capture the dynamic interaction among political parties, the media, and the citizenry.

The design of the last four election studies has been particularly suited to this purpose. These studies have combined a campaign survey with a postelection panel survey and a self-administered mail-back survey. Interviewing for the campaign survey has typically begun almost as soon as the election writs were dropped. The campaign survey has been based on a rolling cross-section design that broke the sample down into daily subsamples that were as similar to each other as random sampling variation permits. Thus differences in vote intentions, information levels, perceptions, and preferences across the daily subsamples largely reflect the impact of the campaign. When combined with a content analysis of the messages conveyed to voters by the political parties and the media during the election campaign, this makes for an extremely powerful design for studying the effects of election campaigns on democratic engagement.

Democratic citizenship is a vast topic and we cannot hope to do it full justice in this book. Indeed, we have made a conscious decision to limit its scope. In particular, we have decided not to include an analysis of the norms and values that underpin democratic citizenship, such as egalitarianism, tolerance, justice, respect for minorities, and empathy. This is not because we consider these unimportant, but, on the contrary, because they could be the subjects of books in themselves. Fortunately, some of the core democratic norms and values — and the tensions among them — have been the examined by Paul Sniderman and his colleagues in *The Clash of Rights* (1996).

Even limiting the focus as we have to interest, involvement, information, and participation, this audit has entailed the analysis of a mass of data. In the interests of accessibility, our results are presented in the form of simple descriptive statistics. It should be emphasized, though, that our conclusions rest on more detailed multivariate analyses. The descriptive statistics enable us to say, for example, how much rich and poor Canadians differ. This is important information in itself, but we also need to know how much of the difference is attributable to disparities in income per se and how much is due to factors, like education, that underlie the income disparities. This is where multivariate analyses come in. They enable us to assess the impact of income (or some other characteristic) when other factors are held constant. Following conventional practice, results are considered to be statistically significant if their probability of occurring by chance is one in twenty or less.

Concluding Comments

There are those who might question the whole notion of auditing democratic citizenship. Indeed, some might construe it as a fundamentally undemocratic exercise. Assessing Canadians' knowledge of politics, in particular, smacks of tests of citizen competence. Marion Smiley has argued powerfully that the very language of competence is tainted. "I worry," she writes, "that the language of citizen competence is inherently antidemocratic" (1999, 372). In her view, judging competence is "part of a larger practice designed to certify particular individuals and to deny certification to others ... The concept of competence must be understood as part of a process through which the participation of some individuals is legitimated and the participation of others is de-legitimated" (pp. 378-9). Smiley's concern is easy to understand. There is an ugly history of standards of competence being used to exclude whole categories of citizens from democratic participation, notably women, the poor, and racial and ethnic minorities. We only have to think of the competency tests that were used to exclude Afro-Americans from exercising the franchise in the American Deep South.

However, the fact that the language of competence has been "used in ways that are not only inimical to democracy but unfair to particular groups" (Smiley 1999, 379) does not mean that the language itself is necessarily antidemocratic. On the contrary, our interest in the nature and extent of citizens' political engagement is motivated by concerns about the inclusiveness and responsiveness of Canadian democracy. Assessing civic competence *can* be motivated by a desire to curtail democracy (and, historically, it too often was), but it can also be motivated by a desire to enhance democracy.

This is the first comprehensive assessment of democratic citizenship in Canada. This book is intended to stimulate debate, not just about the interests and capabilities of Canadians as democratic citizens, but also about the performance of our democratic institutions and the nature of Canadian society. We cannot hope to apportion responsibility for democratic malaise among these various parts, and that is not our intent. We hope instead to stimulate an awareness of the complex interactions among citizens, political institutions, and the structure of Canadian society that together shape the functioning of Canadian democracy.

2 HOW MUCH ATTENTION DO CANADIANS PAY TO POLITICS?

Effective democracies require active and engaged citizens. A crucial prerequisite of an active and engaged citizenry is interest in politics. It is interest, and a dose of civic duty (Blais 2000), that motivate people to devote time and energy to keeping themselves informed about politics. Interest in politics is becoming all the more important given the changes that have occurred in mass communications technology. Before the advent of cable and satellite dishes, Canadian television viewers had a choice of only two television channels. Viewers could hardly avoid coming across at least some news or political programming in the course of their evening's viewing. But in today's multichannel universe, viewers have the option of watching only specialty channels; they can easily avoid news about politics altogether.

Paradoxically, this same revolution in communications technology means that there is more information about politics available in the media than ever before. True news junkies can tune in to nonstop news and public affairs programming. Moreover, citizens are better equipped than ever before to make sense of that information. As in other Western democracies, the "education explosion" (Clark and Rempel 1997) has given Canadians unprecedented access to higher education. If the cognitive mobilization thesis (Inglehart 1990; Dalton 1984) is correct, increasing numbers of citizens should therefore have the skills and the motivation to follow politics closely.

This chapter considers a variety of questions about political interest in the light of this paradox. How much attention do Canadians pay to politics? How many Canadians are interested in politics? How closely do they follow politics in the media? Where do people get most of their information about politics? How often do they talk about politics with others? A key concern is identifying those who are following politics avidly, on the one hand, and those who are tuning out politics altogether, on the other. Then there is the impact of the Internet. Is the explosion of information on-line encouraging tuned-out citizens to start paying more attention to politics, or is it largely benefiting the already cognitively mobilized?

How Much Interest Do Canadians Have in Politics?

Canadians' interest in politics could aptly be described as middling. When the 2000 Canadian Election Study asked Canadians to indicate how interested they were in politics, their average rating on a 0 to 10 scale was 5.9 for interest in the election and 5.5 for interest in politics generally. Almost one Canadian in ten professed no interest at all in politics generally, and 6 percent indicated a total lack of interest in the election. At the other end of the scale, 8 percent said that they were extremely interested in politics generally and 9 percent said that they were extremely interested in the election.

Changes in question wording make it difficult to determine whether interest in politics has been growing or not. Predictably, interest in elections depends very much on the election in question. If we look at Canadian Election Study data for federal elections held between 1974 and 1993, the figures for those who indicated that they were very interested in the election range from lows of 30 percent for the 1974 election and 31 percent for the 1993 election to highs of 39 percent for the 1988 election and 43 percent for the 1980 election. General interest in politics has tended to be more stable. Over the same period, the figures for those saying they followed politics very closely ranged between 14 percent (in 1974 and 1979) and 18 percent (in 1984). The median voter was fairly interested in elections and followed politics in general fairly closely.

By international standards, Canadians actually seem to be more interested in politics than average. At the time of the 1990 World Values Surveys, Canada ranked fourth among seventeen established Western democracies. Average scores on a 0 to 3 scale ranged from a high of 1.87 in the former West Germany to a low of 0.97 in Belgium. Canada was tied with the United States at 1.64, behind West Germany, Switzerland, and Norway. Ten years earlier, Canada had ranked third, with an average score of 1.39, just behind France and West Germany. In both years, the median Canadian voter was somewhat interested in politics.

Who Is Interested in Politics?

Age is the single best predictor of people's political interest. Figure 2.1 compares the average scores of the pre-baby boomers (born before 1945), the baby boomers (born between 1945 and 1959), generation X (born in the 1960s), and post-generation X (born since 1970) on a scale measuring interest in politics in general. The pattern is clear: interest in politics increases with age. This is also true of interest in the 2000 election in particular.

Making sense of such age differences is never easy. At least two interpretations have to be considered: age differences could reflect either life-cycle effects or generational effects. The life-cycle interpretation suggests that young Canadians are less interested in politics simply because they *are* young. People of different ages tend to care about different things. Issues like taxes, interest rates, and access to services are typically not a high priority for young citizens, so political debates that focus on these sorts of issues may seem remote and abstract to many of them. But when young people settle into a job, marry, start a family, or purchase a home, their priorities change, and the politics of taxes, mortgage rates, and government services may

Figure 2.1

Social background and general interest in politics

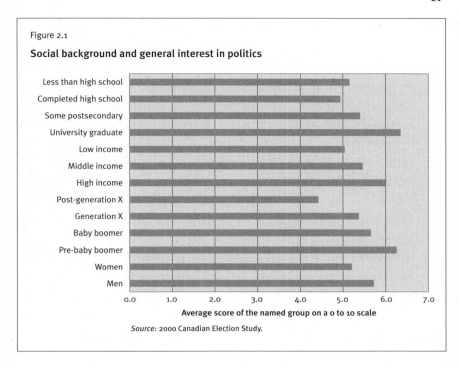

Average score of the named group on a 0 to 10 scale

Source: 2000 Canadian Election Study.

well become more salient. Accordingly, the life-cycle interpretation expects political interest to grow as people get older.

The generational interpretation, on the other hand, argues that people's basic political outlooks, including their interest in politics, depend less on their age than on when they were born. The idea is that people take on the political outlooks that prevailed during their formative years. The generational interpretation of the age differences reported in Figure 2.1 is that young Canadians are less interested in politics because they have grown to adulthood during a period when cynicism about politics was rising, when the ideological mainstream favoured less state intervention, and when globalization seemed to be reducing the capacity of states to manage the economy. This generational explanation has very different implications from the life-cycle explanation. It implies that today's young Canadians are less interested in politics than their parents were when they were young because of generational differences. And because these generational differences affect people for the rest of their lives, the implication is that this generation of Canadians will remain less interested in politics.

To what extent age differences in political interest are a result of life cycle or generational experiences is difficult to determine pre-cisely. The task would be easier if we had cross-time data where the very same questions were repeatedly asked of the very same people over a long period of time. These data are not available, but we can compare people of a similar age at different points in time to see which interpretation is more plausible. In 2000, people born before 1945 were about twice as likely as those born since 1970 to rate their interest in the election at eight or higher on our zero to ten scale. When we compare people in the same age groups in 1974, a similar pattern emerges: those aged over fifty-five were about twice as likely as those aged thirty or less to say that they were very interested in the election. In fact, if the questions are standardized into a common scale, the data are even clearer: the gap between the younger age group and the older age group appears consistently across time for both interest in any given election and interest in politics generally. This seems to suggest a life-cycle effect rather than a generational one.

Political interest is also related to people's material circumstances: the higher Canadians' household income, the more interested in poli-tics they tend to be. The gap between the wealthiest Canadians, those with household incomes in the top 20 percent, and the poorest Canadi-ans, those with household incomes in the bottom 20 percent, is very similar – about one point – for interest in the election and interest in politics in general.

In the case of interest in the election, most of this gap is attribut-able to differences in levels of formal education. The wealthy are more likely to have a university education, and university graduates are typ-ically more interested in politics than the rest of the population. Inter-est in politics tends to be higher among those who have a university degree for at least two reasons. First, a university education provides people with the cognitive skills they need to deal with the complexities of politics. Second, the university experience tends to reinforce norms of civic obligation, which encourage people to take an interest in politics. Once university education is taken into account, income does not make a significant difference to people's interest in the election.

Educational differences, however, are only part of the reason why less affluent Canadians tend to be less interested in politics more generally. Something about living at the economic margins has the effect of depressing political interest. One possibility is that people who have to struggle to make ends meet simply have less time and energy left over to spend following politics. Another possibility is that people at the economic margins are less motivated to take an interest because they believe that the political system does not work very well for them.

Short of being a university graduate, the effects of education are surprisingly modest. The typical high school graduate is no more interested in politics than the typical high school dropout. Only university education makes a significant difference to people's interest in politics.

There are gender differences to consider as well. Women tend to be less interested in politics than men. The gender gap is about half a point for interest in politics in general and a little less for interest in the election. Both gaps are modest, but they are persistent and they cannot be explained away by other social background characteristics: the gender gaps remain even when educational and income differences between men and women are taken into account.

The gender gap in political interest is not a peculiarly Canadian phenomenon. Similar gaps have been observed in other established industrial democracies, and various explanations have been proposed. Early on, lower levels of political interest were often attributed to the fact that women living in traditional family settings spent most of their time at home. However, the gender gaps in political interest have persisted despite the massive influx of women into the paid workforce. Indeed, there is even evidence pointing in the opposite direction. Women who were in full-time employment rated both their interest in the 2000 election and their interest in politics in general half a point lower than women who were full-time homemakers. This partly reflects the fact that women who are full-time homemakers tend to be older. But it undoubtedly also reflects the time demands of the "double day" that many women continue to face. The election study data are revealing on this matter. Men's interest in politics is barely affected by whether or not they have children who live at home. By contrast, women with one or more children under the age of eighteen at home typically rate their interest half a point lower than women who do not have such responsibilities.

As striking as these findings are, they still do not provide a complete or satisfactory account of the gender gap in political interest. One suggestion is that women are less interested in politics because political parties have done so little to stimulate women's interest or encourage their participation (Goot and Reid 1975, 33). Another suggestion is that "women in some part, anyway, consider themselves apolitical because areas which concern them, and which are, indeed, important parts of political debate, such as education and health, are frequently presented as being above 'politics'" (Evans 1980, 221). Then there is the fact that politics remains very much a male activity, one that is both governed and framed by stereotypically masculine norms of behaviour. The language of politics is telling, and the politics-as-sport metaphor seems apt. Elections are depicted as "races," political parties are competing "teams," and differences over issues are "policy battles." Perhaps women simply find the language of conflict less appealing, and the sporting and gladiatorial spectacle less entertaining, than do men. Whatever the cause of the gender gap in political interest, it is not likely to disappear any time soon. Far from narrowing among the younger generation, the gap is actually widest among those born since 1970.

Age, education, income, and gender all go some distance toward explaining variations in political interest. But other factors matter, too. Where people live affects how much interest they have in politics. Residents of Quebec and Saskatchewan are typically less interested (5.0) in politics in general than Canadians at large. Meanwhile, interest is highest in British Columbia (5.8), followed by Manitoba, Ontario, and Newfoundland and Labrador (5.7), and Alberta (5.6). Quebec and Saskatchewan rank lowest in terms of interest in the 2000 federal election as well, but now Quebec (4.8) trails Saskatchewan (5.4) by a significant margin. Even the advent of an avowedly separatist option has not, it seems, induced strong interest in federal electoral politics on the part of Quebeckers. Election interest was highest in Prince Edward Island (6.5), followed by Alberta, Ontario, British Columbia, and Manitoba (6.3). These provincial differences seem to reflect differences in political culture and patterns of partisan competition. Whether people live in rural areas or in cities makes no difference at all; average levels of political interest are very similar.

Finally, people who have come to Canada as immigrants tend to have somewhat higher-than-average levels of interest in both the 2000 election (6.2) and politics in general (5.8). And there is no indication that members of visible minorities are any less interested in politics than the population at large, despite the fact that they remain numerically underrepresented in elected office.

How Much Attention Do Canadians Pay to News about Politics?

In Western industrial democracies, television is the main source of citizens' information about politics (Ansalobehere, Behr, and Iyengar 1993; Dalton 2002). Canada is no exception. The 2000 Canadian Election Study asked Canadians to rate their attention to news about the election on television, on the radio, and in the newspapers, using a scale from 0 to 10. The average rating for attention paid to television news (5.1) was almost one point higher than the average rating for attention to news about the election in the newspapers (4.2), which in turn was almost one point higher than the average rating for news about the election on the radio (3.3). If people pay any attention at all to election news, it is most likely to be on the television. Only one person in ten indicated that they paid no attention whatsoever to news about the election on the television. Meanwhile, one in five paid no attention to election news in the newspapers, and almost one in three paid no attention at all to election news on the radio.

Differences in question wording make it difficult to determine whether, and how, patterns of media usage have been changing. The 1988 and 1993 Canadian Election Studies asked people whether they paid a great deal of attention to news about the election, quite a bit, some, very little, or none. In 1988 only 4 percent replied "none" for news about the election on television and only 11 percent replied "none" for election news in the newspapers. In 1993 the figures were 5 percent and 14 percent, respectively. Attention to news about the election on the radio was not asked in 1988, but in 1993 only 16 percent indicated that they paid no attention. So the number of people who tune out election news altogether may well be increasing.

At the opposite extreme, of course, are the people who qualify as news junkies; they follow the election closely on the television, in the newspapers, and maybe on the radio, too. But which source of information is most important to people? The 2000 Canadian Election Study asked Canadians where they got most of their information about the election: television, radio, newspapers, the Internet, family, or friends. Television won hands down as the main source of information for half of those interviewed (see Figure 2.2). Television received twice as many mentions as newspapers did and more than four times as many mentions as radio. Indeed, almost as many people named family or friends as their main source of information as named radio.

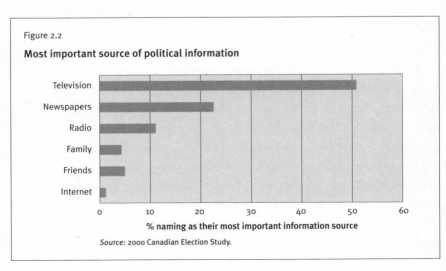

Figure 2.2

Most important source of political information

% naming as their most important information source

Source: 2000 Canadian Election Study.

How Much Attention Do Canadians Pay to Politics?

It is difficult to pinpoint when television assumed its current dominance as a source of political information in Canada. The 1974 Canadian Election Study was the first to ask which source of information was most important to people. However, respondents could choose only among television, newspapers, and radio, and multiple mentions were permitted. Although this measurement approach makes direct comparisons difficult, television had clearly already established itself as the most important source of information. Two in five said television was the most important to them in getting information about politics, and another one in five had television tied with newspapers or radio. Meanwhile, one in three named newspapers as their most important source of information, and almost one in five had newspapers tied with television and/or radio. Even back in 1974, a mere one in twenty relied on radio, and only one in ten had radio tied with television and/or newspapers. While newspapers and television were almost tied with one-third of single mentions each in 1979, television had reestablished a commanding lead (40 percent) by 1984. Only one in seven named newspapers as their most important source of information. A further one in five had newspapers tied with television. Radio fared even worse, with only 3 percent saying it was their most important source of information about the election campaign.

Radio may actually be a more important source of political information today than it was from the mid-1970s to mid-1980s. We can only speculate about the reasons, but one possibility is the rise of "talk radio." The increasing significance of radio could also reflect the swelling ranks of captive commuters who are driving longer distances to work. The more important change, though, is in the relative importance of television and newspapers. Newspapers were a more important source of information in the 1970s than they are today. This change has raised concerns about the quality of political information that Canadians are getting. Henry Milner (2002), in particular, has linked a decline in civic literacy to increasing dependence on commercial television for information about politics. He argues that encouraging newspaper reading would help to promote civic literacy. His thesis gains support from an unexpected quarter; here is what CBC news anchor Peter Mansbridge has had to say:

> Let's not fool ourselves. Most people get news from TV, and that's always bothered me. Sometimes their only source is TV. I know what they're getting. They're not getting enough. We [at the CBC] like to think we take it beyond the headlines because we do documentaries, we go for an hour, we do analysis. But if you take [the script of] an hour-long newscast ... you couldn't fill the front page of your paper (Mansbridge 2002).

Who Reads and Who Watches?

It is all very well to bemoan Canadians' dependence on television as a news source, but the harsh fact is that newspapers are simply not an option for those who lack the requisite literacy skills. The relationship is predictably strong between education and where people turn for information about politics. The less formal schooling people have, the more likely they are to depend on television: three-fifths of those who left school without a high school diploma looked to television as their main source of information about the 2000 election, compared with only two-fifths of university graduates. Meanwhile, university-educated Canadians were twice as likely as high school dropouts to rely primarily on the press (see Figure 2.3). While radio trailed television and newspapers at every level of schooling, university graduates were the most likely (16 percent) to turn to radio as their main source of information about the 2000 election. Conversely, university graduates were the least likely (5 percent) to depend on family and friends for information. Tellingly, even among university graduates television won out over newspapers. The university-educated should be the cognitively mobilized citizens par excellence, and yet many of them opt for the more passive way of following politics.

Given the influence of literacy skills and cognitive abilities on where people look for information, it comes as no surprise to discover

Figure 2.3

Dependence on television and newspapers for information about politics

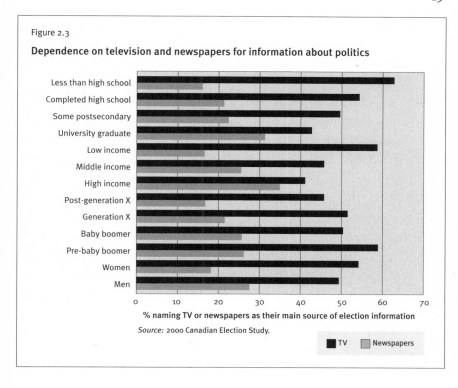

% naming TV or newspapers as their main source of election information

Source: 2000 Canadian Election Study.

■ TV   ▨ Newspapers

that there is a relationship between people's household income and where they turn for their news. The lower people's household income, the less likely they are to rely on newspapers for information and the more likely they are to depend on television. Three-fifths of those from the poorest households named television as their main source of information about the 2000 election, compared with only two-fifths of those from the wealthiest households. Conversely, over one-third of those in the wealthiest households relied on newspapers, compared with only one-sixth of those at the bottom of the economic ladder.

These differences cannot be explained away simply by differences in levels of education; income makes a difference even after education is taken into account. So it is not only weaker literacy skills that make poorer Canadians more reliant on television for political information. Being poor per se affects where people turn for information. One obvious possible reason is the cost of newspapers, which, while low, may be prohibitive for those who have to worry about paying the rent and putting food on the table. Reliance on the radio or on family and friends for political information, by contrast, does not vary much by income.

Another factor to consider is motivation. People who are not very interested in politics are not likely to want to devote time and effort to reading about politics in the newspaper. Television offers them a more passive way of keeping up. Predictably, the profile of those who rely primarily on newspapers for their information resembles the profile of those who are very interested in political matters. Men, for example, are significantly more likely than women to look to newspapers as their main source of information. Similarly, those born before the end of the Second World War are much more likely to rely on newspapers than those born since 1970. Interestingly, young Canadians are the least likely to depend on newspapers and television alike. Instead, fully one in five turn to family and friends for information about politics.

Place of residence also has a strong effect on where people look for political information. At the extremes, close to half of Prince Edward Islanders say that the newspaper is their main source of information, compared with a mere 7 percent of Newfoundlanders. Manitobans (31 percent) and Ontarians (28 percent) are also more likely to rely on the newspaper for news about politics. Meanwhile, Newfoundlanders (80 percent) are the most likely to depend on television, followed at a considerable distance by Quebeckers (60 percent). Prince Edward Islanders (40 percent) are the least dependent on television. Indeed, they make up the one segment of the population that is more likely to rely on newspapers than on television for information about politics. Regardless of their province of residence, rural Canadians are less likely (18 percent) than Canadians at large to say that the newspaper is their main source of information. This may have something to do with availability. In contrast to place of residence, neither country of birth nor racial origin has much effect on where people turn for information about politics, though people who arrived within the past ten years are less likely (15 percent) to rely on the newspaper.

Are Canadians Turning to the Internet for Information about Politics?

The 2000 federal election may well go down in the history books as Canada's first "Internet election." Very few Canadians (1 percent), though, used the Internet as their main source of information about the election (see Figure 2.2). Indeed, only one Canadian in six reported *ever* using the Internet to be informed about politics. In postelection interviews, 13 percent indicated that they had used the Internet to get information about the election. Of these, close to half had visited a political party's website during the campaign.

The implications the Internet revolution might have for democratic citizenship are the subject of a good deal of debate (see Norris 2001; Barney forthcoming 2005). The optimistic view is that the Internet will not only offer citizens new and enhanced possibilities for political engagement but will also draw hitherto marginalized groups into the ranks of the active citizenry. In contrast to this "mobilization hypothesis," the "reinforcement hypothesis" predicts that the new opportunities will largely benefit those who are already politically engaged. The implication of this pessimistic view is that we may experience a growing "digital divide" between "those who do, and do not, use the panoply of digital resources to engage, mobilize and participate in public life" (Norris 2001, 4).

Based on evidence from the United States and the countries of the European Union, Norris (2001) concludes that for now at least there clearly is a digital divide, which she attributes to deep-rooted social inequalities. Internet use requires both financial resources and cognitive skills. The price of home computers has dropped, but purchasing a computer still entails an outlay of funds that is well beyond the means of poorer households. Then there are connection charges and charges for Internet access. Cost is clearly a factor in Canada. According to the 2001 Household Internet Use Survey (Statistics Canada 2002), half of Canadian households had at least one member who used the Internet from home in a typical month. However, rates of Internet use varied substantially across income levels: the vast majority (87 percent) of households with incomes in the top 25 percent contained at least one person who was going on-line, compared with only one-third of households in the bottom 25 percent. Even if people have the financial means, they may lack the cognitive skills to use the new technology. The Internet remains very much a verbal, as opposed to a visual, medium, and users require basic literacy, technology, and language skills, in addition to the abilities necessary to sort through the sheer mass of information available.

Undoubtedly, the costs of the new technology will continue to drop. Just as television sets were once luxury items, but are now found in almost every household, home computers and Internet connectivity will spread through society. But even if we assume that the Internet will sooner or later be available to rich and poor alike, there is reason to be pessimistic about the digital divide. As Norris (2001) argues, tapping into the political resources that are available on-line is not simply a matter of Internet access. Motivation is also crucial. Many Internet users may simply lack the interest to spend time tracking down and visiting political websites. Of course, they may happen upon political information as they surf the net, but this brings us to a crucial difference between the Internet and traditional sources of information about politics, namely the sheer amount of material that is available. People flipping through a newspaper or channel surfing on television are much more likely to encounter information about politics than those who surf the net. And far from surfing aimlessly, many Internet users are searching for particular types of content. This is why Norris is pessimistic about the Internet's potential to mobilize people politically: "As the media of choice *par excellence* it is difficult to know how the Internet *per se* can ever reach the civically disengaged" (p. 231).

A clear digital divide exists in Canada in the use of the Internet to get information about politics (see Figure 2.4). The single most important factor defining this divide is education. Almost a third of university graduates have used the Internet to be informed about politics. That figure plummets to one in twenty for those with less than a high school education. Household income is also a factor. People with

Figure 2.4

The digital divide

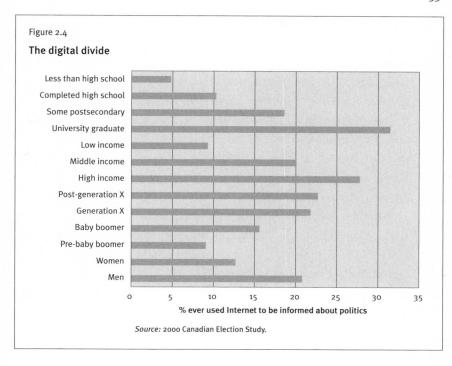

% ever used Internet to be informed about politics

Source: 2000 Canadian Election Study.

household incomes in the top 20 percent are about three times as likely to have used the Internet to get information about politics as people with household incomes in the bottom 20 percent, and household income continues to have an effect even when differences in educational attainment are taken into account. There is also a gender gap: men are much more likely than women to be using the Internet to keep up with politics.

In these respects, the profile of people who go on-line in search of information about politics is very similar to the profile of people who rely on newspapers as their chief source of information. There is one major exception: predictably, younger Canadians are much more likely than older Canadians to have used the Internet to track down political information. Understandably, hopes have been high that the Internet will help to counteract the tendency of young Canadians to tune out of politics, but this optimism might not be warranted. True, the Internet is the one source of political information used most heavily by the young, but those young Canadians who are the most likely to be following politics in conventional media are also the most likely to be going on-line to get information about politics. Among those born since 1970, the Internet users scored fully two points higher on average than nonusers for attention to both television news and news in the newspaper (on a scale from 0 to 10). This is not surprising, since university graduates are the most likely (38 percent) to go on-line for this purpose. In contrast, only 8 percent of young Canadians who left school without a high school diploma have ever used the Internet to get information about politics.

Whether people were born in Canada makes little difference to their propensity to go on-line for political information. What does matter is how long they have lived in Canada. People who arrived within the last thirty years are much more likely to use the Internet to get political information. This Internet usage may simply be a by-product of this group's desire to keep up with politics in countries where they still have family ties and which typically receive little coverage in Canadian newspapers. This same desire may also help to explain why members of visible minorities have a significantly higher rate (28 percent) of Internet use. Tellingly, place of origin had much less impact when it came to using the Internet to get information about the 2000 federal election.

Patterns of Internet use reveal other differences. Rural Canadians are somewhat less likely (12 percent) than Canadians in general to have gone on-line to get political information, but the urban-rural difference disappears once other social background characteristics are taken into account. Province matters more than type of community. The figures range from around 10 percent in Prince Edward Island, Saskatchewan, and Quebec to around 20 percent in Ontario, Alberta, and British Columbia. This may partly reflect provincial variations in the percentage of wired households. According to the Household Internet Use Survey (Statistics Canada 2002), British Columbia, Ontario, and Alberta have the highest rates of Internet use at a little over 50 percent. However, while Newfoundland and Labrador ranks lowest in terms of household Internet use (36 percent), in the 2000 Canadian

Election Study fully 18 percent of Newfoundlanders reported that they had gone on-line for information about politics. This is not so surprising: as we saw above, Newfoundlanders tend to be more interested in politics than the average Canadian.

Indeed, motivation is a key correlate of the digital divide. People who use the Internet to retrieve political information tend to be more interested in politics than nonusers. On a zero to ten scale, the difference is almost one and three-quarter points. One possibility is that people who surf the Net happen upon some political information and this information piques their interest in politics. It seems much more likely, though, that the Internet serves mainly "to engage the engaged" (Norris 2001, 22). Norris likens the relationship between political engagement and accessing political information on the Internet to a "virtuous circle": political interest motivates citizens to go on-line in search of political information in the first place, and that interest is reinforced as political awareness and knowledge of politics deepen in consequence. What is clear is that the Internet supplements rather than supplants other sources of political information. People who have gone on-line in search of political information score significantly higher than average when it comes to attention to news on television (5.8) and news in the newspaper (5.3). For the present at least, it is difficult to argue that the Internet is serving to arouse a new interest in politics among the politically unaware.

How Often Do Canadians Talk about Politics?

Some of the pioneering work on the impact of the media on opinion found that personal communication had more influence than the media (Lazarsfeld, Berelson, and Gaudet 1948). To the extent that the media did have an effect, it was typically at one step removed, via discussions with "opinion leaders." The opinion leaders were people who followed politics closely and passed on what they had learned in conversations with family, friends, neighbours, and colleagues. As we have seen, interpersonal communication remains important. Almost one in every ten Canadians named family or friends as their *main* source of information about the 2000 federal election (see Figure 2.2). This figure rose to one in five among those born since 1970.

Political discussion is the one expression of interest in politics that cuts across age groups (see Figure 2.5). Those born since 1970 discussed the 2000 federal election with other people almost as often as those born before 1945 did. Aside from age, though, the pattern is a familiar one: education, income, and gender differences are clear. People with less than a high school education were much less likely to have frequent conversations about the election than university graduates. Similarly, poorer Canadians discussed the election less often than their affluent counterparts, and these differences persisted even when education was taken into account. Finally, women discussed the election less frequently than did men.

In short, the people who could benefit most from the two-step flow of information seem to be the least likely to engage in conversations about politics. The one exception is young Canadians, for some of

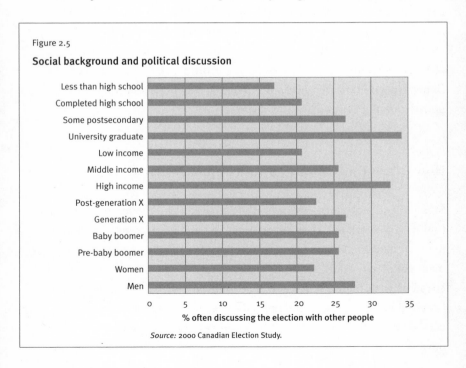

Figure 2.5

Social background and political discussion

% often discussing the election with other people

Source: 2000 Canadian Election Study.

whom, at least, chats with family and friends provide a way of keeping up with politics. In general, though, talking about politics is simply another way that people who are already interested in politics express that interest. For example, people who said that they often discussed the election with other people rated their interest in politics much higher (7.0) than those who discussed the election only occasionally (5.4) or not at all (3.7). Similarly, they paid much more attention to news about the election on television and in the newspapers.

The amount of political discussion that goes on varies from one part of the country to another. Residents of Saskatchewan (15 percent), Quebec (20 percent), and New Brunswick (20 percent) were the least likely to engage in frequent discussions about the 2000 federal election. Meanwhile, Albertans (35 percent) seemed to talk about it a good deal. Counter to stereotype, rural Canadians were no more likely to engage in political chat than urban Canadians. Nor was there any difference between citizens born in Canada and those born abroad. Canadians who belong to visible minorities, however, were less likely (18 percent) to have frequent conversations about the election than Canadians in general, and this difference persisted even after other social characteristics were taken into account.

These differences in the frequency of political discussion are telling, but there is a larger point to be made: for the majority of Canadians, politics typically enters only occasionally into conversation. University graduate or high school dropout, rich or poor, man or woman, young or old, 60 percent or more of Canadians said that they only occasionally discussed the 2000 election with other people.

No evidence indicates that people discuss politics more frequently now than before. In 1974, 30 percent of people interviewed after the federal election indicated that they had often discussed the election with other people, while 14 percent said that they had never discussed the election. Interviewed after the 1984 federal election, 24 percent said that they often discussed politics with other people, while 14 percent said that they never did. In 2000, 25 percent of those interviewed after the election reported that they had often discussed the election with other people, while 12 percent said that they had not discussed it at all.

Still, Canada seems to rank above the median for established Western democracies. According to the 1990 World Values Surveys, 19 percent of Canadians discussed politics frequently, which put Canada in fifth place, behind the former West Germany (which ranked first with 25 percent), Denmark, Norway, and Austria. Politics was discussed least often in Finland and Spain (10 percent) and Belgium (9 percent).

Discussion

A core of cognitively mobilized Canadians are clearly interested in politics and pay a good deal of attention to what is going on in public life. Higher education is only one of the characteristics that define the politically engaged. Income also affects how much attention people pay to politics, and it does so independently of educational attainment. The same is true of gender. Women simply do not follow politics as closely as men, and this cannot be explained away by the fact that women are less likely than men to be university graduates and tend to have lower incomes than men. In fact, the gender gap is typically wider for university-educated women and for affluent women.

Equally clearly, many Canadians have little interest in politics and pay scant attention to the news. Some commentators have expressed high hopes that the Internet would enhance political interest and re-engage some of these Canadians who have been tuning out of politics. But that optimistic vision remains unfulfilled. Rather than increasing the political awareness of poorer, less educated Canadians, Internet usage provides an additional source of information for those who already pay close attention to politics. The one apparent exception relates to age: younger Canadians are more likely than older Canadians to use the Internet to get political information. However, it is disproportionately the university-educated who go on-line for this purpose, rather than young Canadians in general. Those who are tuned out do not use the Internet to tune in.

Similarly, there is no indication that political discussion serves as an alternative source of information for people who are not following politics in the media. If people are not interested in politics to begin with, politics is unlikely to be a frequent topic of conversation. Once again, young Canadians are something of an exception: as many as one in five rely on family and friends as their primary source of information about politics.

Higher education and access to multiple sources of political information clearly enhance people's attention to politics. However, we should not overstate the importance of cognitive mobilization. Even university-educated Canadians are more likely to get most of their news about politics from watching television rather than reading a newspaper. And even university-educated Canadians are unlikely to engage more than occasionally in discussions about politics.

Chapter 2

◆ Canadians' interest in politics is best described as middling.

◆ Men, university graduates, and affluent Canadians are the most interested in politics and pay the most attention to news about politics in the media.

◆ Canadians' main source of information about politics is television. Even university graduates are more likely to rely on television than on newspapers for their political news.

◆ Young Canadians are less interested in politics and follow politics less closely than older Canadians. They are the most likely to rely on family and friends for information about politics.

◆ The Internet serves mainly as an additional source of information for people who already pay attention to politics.

◆ Younger, educated Canadians are the most likely to go on-line for information about politics.

◆ For the majority of Canadians, politics is only an occasional topic of conversation.

WHAT DO CANADIANS KNOW ABOUT POLITICS?

3

To become Canadian citizens, people have to pass a citizenship test designed to assess their knowledge of "Canada's history, geography, system of government and the rights and responsibilities of citizenship" (Citizenship and Immigration Canada 2002). If this test is the benchmark for assessing democratic citizenship, the Canadian public falls woefully short. According to a Canada Day 2001 poll for Global TV and the *Ottawa Citizen,* four in five Canadians would fail (COMPAS 2001). When asked ten questions selected from the test battery, only 17 percent of those surveyed got a passing grade. Almost as many (14 percent) failed to get a single answer correct. Another 14 percent managed just one correct response.

This chapter focuses on Canadians' knowledge of current Canadian politics. How many Canadians know such straightforward facts as the names of the federal party leaders or their provincial premier? How many are familiar with where Canada's political parties stand on the issues of the day? Who are the "information rich" and who are the "information poor"? Do election campaigns help the information poor to fill in the gaps in their knowledge? Can Canadians tell left from right, politically speaking?

CAN YOU PASS THE CITIZENSHIP TEST?

Who are the Métis ... and from whom are they descended?

What important trade or commerce did the Hudson's Bay Company control during the early settlement of Canada?

Which group of people played a major role in physically building the Canadian Pacific Railway across the west?

When did the British North America Act come into effect?

Which four provinces first formed the Confederation?

Which province is the only officially bilingual province?

Parliament created a new territory in Canada's North. What is the name of the new territory?

What does one call the Queen's representative in the provinces and territories?

What does one call a law before it is passed?

How many electoral districts are there in Canada?

To see how you did, go to "A look at Canada," study guide, <www.cic.gc. ca/english/citizen/look/look-ooe.html>. A survey of test results is available at <www.compas.ca/data/010621-CitizenshipPollForGlobal-P.pdf>.

Knowing Who's Who in Canadian Politics

The names of key political players are a very basic form of political knowledge. In a federal election, the most prominent political actors are the leaders of the federal political parties; they are "the superstars of Canadian politics" (Clarke et al. 1991, 89). The media focus so much on party leaders that if a leader takes a day off from the campaign, his or her party may well receive no coverage on that night's newscast (Mendelsohn 1993). The televised leaders' debates, which are typically held midway through the campaign, also put the spotlight on the party leaders. This emphasis on the party leaders is easy to understand: the leader of the winning party will become the country's prime minister.

So, how many Canadians were able to name each of the party leaders by the time that the 2000 federal election was over? The answer depends very much on the particular leader and his or her party (see Figure 3.1). The best known was Liberal Party leader Jean Chrétien. This is hardly surprising; Chrétien had been in elected office for more than thirty years and was the incumbent prime minister. More surprising, perhaps, is that fully one in ten of those interviewed could *not* come up with his name. Fewer than three in five were able to name Alexa McDonough as leader of the New Democratic Party (NDP) even though she was contesting her second federal election as party leader. Length of time on the federal political scene is actually rather a poor predictor of a leader's familiarity to voters. Stockwell Day had only been the Alliance leader for a few months, whereas Conservative leader Joe Clark was a former prime minister, but Day was the better known.

Canadians differed in their familiarity with the party leaders. One way to gauge this variation is by the number of leaders people could name. People outside Quebec were not asked to name the leader of the Bloc Québécois, so, for the sake of comparability, we consider the

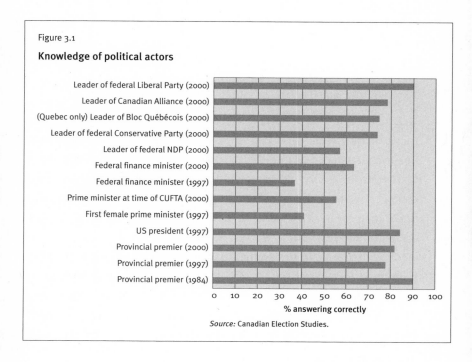

Figure 3.1

Knowledge of political actors

Source: Canadian Election Studies.

responses for the Liberal, Alliance, and Conservative party leaders, plus the Bloc leader in Quebec and the NDP leader outside Quebec (the NDP received less than 2 percent of the Quebec vote). Over half (56 percent) of those interviewed right after the election got the names of all four party leaders right, but fully a quarter were able to come up with only one or two correct names and 7 percent came up with none.

There is very little cross-time data measuring Canadians' knowledge of the federal party leaders. The one available benchmark comes from a survey conducted in conjunction with the Royal Commission on Electoral Reform and Party Financing (the Lortie Commission) in 1990 (Blais and Gidengil 1991). Respondents were asked to name the prime minister of Canada and the leaders of the federal Liberal Party and the federal NDP. While 95 percent of those surveyed were able to come up with the name of Conservative prime minister Brian Mulroney, knowledge levels dropped off precipitously for Liberal leader Jean Chrétien (57 percent) and especially for NDP leader Audrey McLaughlin (33 percent). These figures suggest that, for many Canadians, the opposition party leaders are simply off the radar screen when an election is not in progress. While Chrétien had been the leader of the Liberal Party for only two or three months at the time of the survey, he hardly qualified as a new face on the federal scene, having served as a minister in the Trudeau government as far back as 1969. Meanwhile, McLaughlin had been her party's leader for over nine months.

Like the 2000 Canadian Election Study results discussed above, an Institute for Research on Public Policy (IRPP) survey conducted early in 2000 suggests that knowledge levels may actually be falling (Howe and Northrup 2000). When asked to name the prime minister, fully one in ten were unable to come up with Jean Chrétien's name. And only one Canadian in three knew that the Reform Party was the Official Opposition in Ottawa.

After the prime minister, the finance minister is probably the most prominent member of the federal cabinet. Yet, when interviewed after the 1997 federal election, fewer than two Canadians in five could identify Paul Martin as the federal finance minister, the person responsible for charting the nation's fiscal and monetary course (see Figure 3.1). To put this figure in context, consider that more than twice as many Canadians could name the president of the United States (Bill Clinton). By the time of the IRPP survey in early 2000, more people (46 percent) had managed to learn Paul Martin's name, but despite the attention given in the media to the rivalry between the finance minister and the prime minister, over one-third of those interviewed at the time of the election in the fall were still unable to come up with his name. Within four months of the election, barely one Canadian in two (47 percent) was able to recall the finance minister's name (CRIC0103).

The public's knowledge of former prime ministers was even sketchier. In 1997 fewer than three Canadians in five recalled that Brian Mulroney was the prime minister at the time the Canada-US Free Trade Agreement (CUFTA) was signed. And by the time of the 2000 federal election, only two in five could recall that Kim Campbell was the first woman to become prime minister of Canada. It might be objected that this sort of knowledge is inconsequential, of relevance only to trivia buffs, but it signifies a general lack of political awareness and, as we shall see, this can be consequential.

The focus so far has been on federal politics. Are knowledge levels any higher when we turn to provincial political figures? Given the decentralized nature of the Canadian federal system, provincial premiers are important political actors. At the time of the 2000 federal election, though, almost one Canadian in five was unable to name the premier of their province (see Figure 3.1). This was a slight improvement over the 1997 figure, but provincial premiers were clearly less well known to Canadians than they had been at the time of the 1984 federal election. Although it is tempting to interpret this change as indicating that Canadians are becoming increasingly ignorant about things political, there are reasons to be cautious about drawing such a conclusion. The 1984 Canadian Election Study involved face-to-face interviews with respondents in their own homes, whereas the recent election studies have been based on telephone interviews. Telephone interviews may make it harder for respondents to scan the more remote recesses of their memory to come up with a name. More important, the 1984 federal election took place at a time when provincial premiers were more prominent actors on the national political stage. This was an era of "province-building" (Young, Faucher, and Blais 1984), when assertive premiers were attempting to wrest more power from the federal government. The election also marked the end of a period of such contentious federal government initiatives as the National Energy Program and the repatriation of the constitution, which had helped to make federal-provincial conflicts a staple of the daily news.

At the time of the 2000 federal election, Albertans proved to be the most familiar with their premier: 90 percent were able to name Premier Ralph Klein. The recognition rate had been similarly high (88 percent) in the province in 1997. Residents of Quebec and Prince Edward Island also scored high in 2000. Eighty-eight percent of Quebeckers were able to name Premier Lucien Bouchard, and 88 percent of Prince Edward Islanders knew Pat Binns' name. Surprisingly, though, only 82 percent of Quebeckers had been able to come up with Bouchard's name in 1997, despite his prominent role in bringing the 'yes' side so close to victory in the 1995 Quebec referendum on sovereignty. In 2000 the recognition rates were lowest for John Hamm in Nova Scotia (68 percent), Ujjal Dosanjh in British Columbia (69 percent), Gary Doer in Manitoba (72 percent), and Bernard Lord in New Brunswick (73 percent). Not coincidentally, these four premiers had been in office only a relatively short time, ranging from seventeen months for Lord to only nine months for Dosanjh. This is confirmed by the fact that the recognition rates were much higher in 1997 for Frank McKenna in New Brunswick (88 percent) and Gary Filmon in Manitoba (87 percent). Both premiers had been in office for nine years. Meanwhile, the recognition rate was much lower for British Columbia's Glen Clark (71 percent) who had been in office for only fifteen months. The exception to this pattern is Nova Scotia, where only 74 percent came up with the name of John Savage, even though he had been the province's premier since 1993.

In the 1984 Canadian Election Study, respondents were asked to name all ten provincial premiers. The median number of correct responses was three. Since one of the correct responses was typically the name of the respondent's own premier, this means that the typical Canadian knew the names of the premiers of two other provinces. The best-known premiers at the time were Quebec's René Lévesque and Ontario's Bill Davis (see Lambert et al. 1988). Almost three-quarters of Canadians living outside Quebec were able to name Lévesque, while half of those living outside Ontario got Davis's name correct.

Lambert and his colleagues (1988) found that, once factors like income, education, and political engagement were taken into account, residents of the Atlantic provinces were significantly better informed than other Canadians about the names of the premiers. They linked this regional variation to disparities in political clout, an interpretation that is consistent with Canadians' ability to recall the name of the president of the United States. This "metropolitan-hinterland" interpretation recognizes the relations of dominance and dependence that exist among the regions of Canada (see, for example, Clement 1978; Matthews 1983; Gidengil 1989). From this perspective, it is hardly surprising that Atlantic Canadians were typically able to name more premiers than the residents of other regions. Residents of hinterland provinces have both the opportunity and the incentive to find out what is happening in other parts of Canada. They are more likely to encounter news about the populous and powerful provinces than residents of those provinces are to encounter news about one or another of the Atlantic provinces. And their economic dependence on the wealthier provinces gives residents of Atlantic Canada a reason to pay attention to news about those provinces.

Once we look beyond the premier, knowledge of provincial political actors appears to be sparse. At the time of the 1989 Quebec provincial election, Quebeckers were asked to name two or three candidates of the Parti Québécois, besides the party's leader, Jacques Parizeau. Only one Quebecker in three was able to come up with at least one name (CR8909A). We cannot be sure that knowledge levels would be similarly low in other provinces, but we have no reason to believe that Quebeckers would be less informed than average about provincial politics. Indeed, we should expect the reverse.

It is often argued that municipal politics is closer to citizens. This is true, of course, in a strictly geographical sense, but the argument goes beyond mere physical proximity. Municipalities are responsible for such things as street lighting, the provision of libraries and recreational activities, garbage collection, and public safety, which impinge very directly on people's well being. This line of reasoning suggests that people may pay more attention to what is going on in municipal politics than they do to what is happening in Ottawa or in their provincial capital.

Again, the evidence on this score comes from Quebec. When interviewed by CROP in the run-up to the 1990 municipal election, almost nine Montrealers in ten were able to name Jean Doré when asked to identify the city's mayor (CR9010). This is comparable to the number of people who are able to name the prime minister of Canada or the premier of their province. Again, though, there is a steep drop-off in knowledge once we look beyond the chief executive. In the same survey, Montrealers were asked whether they knew the name of their city councillor or had ever heard about him or her. Not even a third could answer in the affirmative, despite there being a municipal election in the offing and despite the fact that they were not even required to come up with a name. To judge by these results, executive dominance actually seems to increase, at least in terms of visibility, as we move from the federal to the provincial to the municipal level. The municipal parties fared a little better, or at least the dominant party did. Half of those interviewed were able to come up with the name of at least one of Montreal's municipal parties.

How Canadians' knowledge about politics rates by international standards is extremely difficult to assess, because it is so hard to come up with equivalent questions across countries. However, Henry Milner (2002) has compiled some data on knowledge of international affairs. According to a survey conducted in January 1994 by the Times-Mirror Center for the People and the Press, Canada ranked fourth among five countries with an average of 1.90 correct answers out of a possible five, ahead of the United States (1.67), but behind Britain (2.07), France (2.13), and Germany (3.58). Canada fared similarly poorly on a survey that asked respondents to identify the UN secretary general from a list of five names and to name one UN agency. Among the fourteen countries surveyed, only Ireland and the United States performed more poorly than Canada.

Who Knows Most and Who Knows Least?

Political knowledge is not distributed evenly across the population (see also Fournier 2002). It is not simply that some Canadians know less about politics than others. Rather, Canadians sharing particular background characteristics have *systematically* lower levels of political knowledge than their fellow citizens. Given the socially uneven distribution of political interest and attention documented in the previous chapter, this finding comes as little surprise.

We can get a clearer sense of which characteristics differentiate the information rich from the information poor by considering how Canadians were distributed across a scale created from responses to four general political knowledge questions in the 2000 Canadian Election Study. Respondents were asked to name their provincial premier, the federal finance minister, the prime minister at the time of the Canada-US Free Trade Agreement, and the capital of the United States. As we saw in Figure 3.1, on the first three questions, the percentage of correct answers ranged from 56 percent for former prime minister Brian Mulroney to 82 percent for the premier of the respondent's province. Eighty-four percent were able to name Washington, DC. However, only two Canadians in five were able to answer all four questions correctly. At the other extreme, one in twenty failed to answer a single question, and another one in ten managed only one correct answer. The median number of correct answers was three out of the possible four. The intriguing question is whether there were systematic differences between the kinds of people who scored high and those who scored low.

The single most important characteristic that distinguished those who knew less from those who knew more was education (see Figure 3.2).

Figure 3.2

Social background and general knowledge about politics

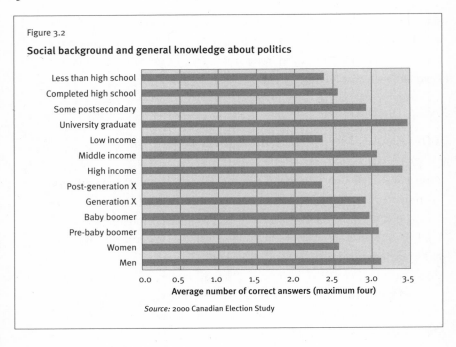

Average number of correct answers (maximum four)

Source: 2000 Canadian Election Study

The more education people had, the more political facts they got right. The typical university graduate got at least one more correct answer than the typical person whose education ended without a high school diploma. This was also true of knowledge of the party leaders.

Education affects general knowledge about politics for a number of reasons. First, people's level of formal education is a good indication of their general propensity to acquire information. Second, education enhances people's cognitive capabilities, making it easier for them to acquire and interpret information (Delli Carpini and Keeter 1996). These capabilities include both literacy skills and facility in integrating information. Educational attainment is also likely to be associated with social roles where information about politics comes in useful and with participation in social networks where information about politics is likely to circulate (see Tichenor, Donohue, and Olien 1970). People who are more highly educated are more likely to have conversations with people who are well informed about what is going on in the news. These conversations provide an opportunity to learn about politics, as well as an incentive to acquire information in order to be able to converse knowledgeably. In short, education seems to affect people's motivation and ability to acquire new information and to integrate it into their existing stock of information.

Alternatively, these differences in political knowledge may reflect people's material circumstances rather than their level of education per se. People with less education tend to be poorer, and people who are poorer generally know less about politics. The poorest Canadians typically got at least one fewer question right than their wealthy counterparts. There was a similar difference in knowledge of party leaders. As discussed in Chapter 2, material circumstances affect people's politics. Simply providing for their basic needs may leave poor Canadians with little time or energy to follow politics. And if they sense that the political system is not particularly responsive to their needs and concerns, they may feel that there is little point in paying close attention to what is going on politically. The more affluent, by contrast, have both the resources and the perceived stake to keep abreast of politics.

In fact, education and income each have some independent effect on general knowledge about politics. Affluence can only partially compensate for lack of formal schooling. Conversely, higher education can attenuate, but not eliminate, the effects of material disadvantage. So differences in political knowledge reflect both cognitive skills and material circumstances.

Neither of these differences, however, explains why women tend to know less about politics than men. Women who had completed some postsecondary education were no better informed than men who had not completed high school. And women with household incomes in the top 20 percent were no better informed than men from middle-income households. Clearly, we have to look elsewhere to explain the gender gap in political knowledge.

Like their lower levels of political interest, women's lower levels of political knowledge used to be attributed to their traditional role as wives and mothers, which often kept them tied to the home. And in 2000 women who were full-time homemakers typically did get fewer questions right: only two correct responses on average. However, full-time homemakers are very much a minority among women today, and the fact remains that women who were in full-time paid employment were typically less informed (2.6) than the average man (3.1). Married or single, the difference in men's and women's political knowledge persists. Women who were married or living with a partner knew more about politics than women who had never married, but this was true of men as well. Childcare responsibilities do not seem to be responsible, either. Women with children under the age of eighteen living at home were only slightly less knowledgeable, on average, than other women. This was even true of women in full-time employment. So the gender gap in political knowledge cannot be explained by the greater demands on women's time.

This gender gap is not a peculiarly Canadian phenomenon. Similar findings have been reported in other settings (Nadeau, Niemi, and Levine 1993; Delli Carpini and Keeter 1996; Verba, Burns, and Schlozman 1997). In Canada, as elsewhere, this gender gap in political knowledge mirrors an underlying gap in political interest (see Chapter 2). Verba and his colleagues suggest that both are "a reflection of the fact that politics has been traditionally, and continues to be, dominated by men" (p. 1053). If so, the presence of significantly more women in elected office will likely be necessary to close the gender gap in political knowledge. Tellingly, the gender gap did not disappear when women were asked to name the leader of the federal NDP and the first woman prime minister of Canada. By the end of the 2000 federal election campaign, only 51 percent of women knew Alexa McDonough's name, compared with 62 percent of men. The gap was narrower for Kim Campbell, but men (43 percent) still had an edge over women (39 percent) when this question was posed at the time of the 1997 federal election.

In fact, differences in political interest or in the amount of attention paid to the news do not explain the gender gap in political knowledge. Men with little or no interest in politics still managed to answer as many questions correctly as women with a middling amount of interest. Similarly, men who paid only a middling amount of attention to news about politics in the press seemed to know more than women who indicated that they paid a good deal of attention. This pattern is repeated for radio and television.

Many feminist scholars might question the sort of items that have been used to assess women's political knowledge. According to Smiley (1999, 380), for example, those who set the standards typically do not ask what citizenship means to the people whose competence they are evaluating, nor do they ask *them* "what kinds of political skills are required to be a competent, not to mention good, citizen." Smiley's challenge builds on the fact that the standards typically derive from a conception of politics that limits itself to the traditional arenas of political engagement (electoral politics, party politics, legislative politics, interest group politics, and so on). In encouraging readers to conceive of political knowledge and democratic citizenship more broadly, she gives the example of ability to obtain welfare assistance for one's family: "What might appear competent to a welfare mother, for example, [is] obtaining welfare services for her children" (p. 382). Conventional conceptions would simply not recognize "welfare recipience as a site of politics" (p. 382) and would, in consequence, underestimate this woman's political competence.

The ability to access such entitlements is undoubtedly an important skill and one of much more immediate material consequence to the woman and her family than any amount of knowledge of politics as traditionally conceived. This type of argument, however, seems to overlook the relevance of traditional political arenas for determining such fundamental questions as who is entitled to welfare assistance and how much should be allocated to the provision of such assistance. These questions may seem remote from the life of a woman who is struggling to make ends meet, but they are, in fact, of crucial importance to her well-being and that of her family.

Tellingly, the one area of politics about which women appear to be better informed than men is school board politics. According to a 1990 CROP survey in Quebec, for example, women were more likely than men to know the date of the next school board elections and to know the name of at least one of their school board commissioners (CR9011B). They were also more likely to have voted in school board elections. Apparently, school board politics are more salient to women than they are to men. This seems to be true in the United States as well (Verba, Burns, and Schlozman 1997). Verba and his colleagues suggest that school board politics has traditionally been more hospitable to women. It could also be that this is an area of politics that touches very directly on the day-to-day preoccupations of women with preschool and school-age children. Still, only a minority of women in the CROP survey were able to answer the school board questions correctly.

Like their counterparts in the United States (Nadeau, Niemi, and Levine 1993; Delli Carpini and Keeter 1996), young Canadians typically know less about politics. Their low level of general knowledge about politics could be attributable to the simple fact that they *are* young. They have had less exposure to the world of politics and less time to store up political information. But this does not explain why they were significantly less likely than older Canadians to know the name of the leader of the Canadian Alliance, which was a new party with a new leader in 2000.

It is tempting to dismiss the apparent political ignorance on the part of many young Canadians. Perhaps they find electoral politics irrelevant to their real concerns. Certainly, they are less interested in what is going on than older Canadians, so it is hardly surprising that the young do not seem well informed about the main actors. The implication of this line of argument is clear: if we just asked the right questions, we would uncover much higher levels of knowledge on the part of the young. Unfortunately, this does not seem to be the case. In March 2001 the Centre for Research and Information on Canada conducted a survey to probe Canadians' views about globalization and free trade (CRIC0103). If there is one topic that should be of special interest to the young, it is globalization, or so popular commentary would have us believe. However, only 57 percent of Canadians born since 1970 had heard anything about globalization, only 53 percent had heard anything about the demonstrations against the World Trade Organization that had taken place the previous year in Seattle, and a paltry 40 percent had heard anything about the upcoming Summit of the Americas in Quebec City. On all three questions, awareness was lowest among the young. Seventy four percent of baby boomers had heard about globalization, 71 percent had heard about the Seattle demonstrations, and 57 percent were aware of the upcoming summit. Even Canadians born before 1945 seemed to know more about what was going on than did young people. Their figures were 63 percent for globalization, 66 percent for the Seattle demonstrations, and 61 percent for the summit.

Whether Canadians are citizens by birth seems to make little difference to how much they know about Canadian politics. The only exception is newcomers. Canadians who had been in Canada for ten years or less at the time of the 2000 federal election were typically able to come up with fewer correct answers (2.3) than Canadians at large (2.9). Part of the explanation may be the sheer demands that are placed on people's time and energies as they seek to establish themselves in a new and different setting. Once established, though, people who have been here for more than ten years are basically indistinguishable from the population at large when it comes to their general political knowledge. Canadians who belong to a visible minority tended to be a little less well informed (2.6), but the differences were not substantial.

Atlantic Canadians typically got fewer answers correct, which partly reflects the lower income and education levels in the region. On the whole, though, place of residence made little difference to people's general political knowledge: the average number of correct answers ranged from a low of 2.5 in Newfoundland and Labrador and New Brunswick to a high of 3.0 in Alberta. Nova Scotians were the most knowledgeable (3.5) when it came to naming the party leaders, but this can be attributed to the fact that the least well known of the leaders – the NDP's Alexa McDonough – came from Nova Scotia, and 83 percent of the province's residents knew her name. Similarly, 92 percent of Albertans knew that the province's former treasurer, Stockwell Day, was the Alliance leader. Whether people lived in a rural community or an urban area seemed to make little difference to the number of correct answers they came up with.

Predictably, the more interested people were in politics, the more answers they knew. Similarly, the more attention they paid to the news, the more knowledgeable they were. Whether they were listening to news on the radio, watching the news on television, or reading about politics in the newspaper made little difference when it came to answering these straightforward factual questions.

Some associate low levels of political knowledge with high levels of television viewing (Milner 2001). That may hold true at the aggregate level across countries, but according to data from the 2000 Canadian Election Study, it does not seem to hold at the individual level within Canada. Whether they were watching television three hours a day or more or one hour a day or less made little difference to people's general political knowledge. What did make a significant difference was the frequency of newspaper reading (cf. Milner 2001). People who read a newspaper only once a week, or less, typically got fewer correct answers (2.6) than those who read a newspaper six or seven days a week (3.3). And people who indicated that they got most of their information about the 2000 federal election from the newspapers tended to be somewhat better informed (3.2) than those who relied primarily on television (2.8). The least useful sources of information about the election seemed to be family and friends: people who relied primarily on one or the other for their information averaged only two correct responses.

The important point to emphasize is that media use had an impact regardless of people's level of education. Even if they had left school without a high school diploma, people who reported paying a good deal of attention to news in the newspaper typically got more answers correct (2.9) than those who paid little or no attention (2.2). The same was true of those who paid a good deal of attention to television news. In neither case, though, did increased attention to the news make up for the disadvantages of a lack of formal schooling. Even when they reported paying the same amount of attention to news on television or in the newspaper, those with less education typically knew less than those with more education. The gap was only a little narrower among those who were avid viewers or readers. Meanwhile, paying attention to news about politics on the radio did little to compensate for lack of schooling. University graduates who paid little or no attention to news on the radio knew significantly more (3.4) than people who paid a good deal of attention but had not completed high school (2.6). That finding is significant because it implies that education does more than enhance people's interest in politics or encourage them to pay more attention to the news. Formal schooling also equips people with the cognitive skills that help them to assimilate what they read and hear.

People who talked about politics with other people were better informed than those who did not. The average number of correct responses to the factual questions ranged from 3.4 for those who had often discussed the election with others to only 2.1 for those who had not talked about it at all. The gap was, if anything, even wider when it came to naming the party leaders. There are at least two reasons why people who discuss politics might know more. First, these conversations are likely to be a source of information about politics, and second, if people know they are likely to be discussing politics they have an incentive to inform themselves.

Finally, people who had used the Internet to get information about the election tended to be more knowledgeable (3.3) than average. This was true of knowledge of the parties' leaders as well, whether or not the Internet users had actually visited a party's website. However, only a tiny minority (1.2 percent) of those interviewed said that they had got most of their information about the election from the Internet. On average, they came up with correct answers to three of the four general factual information questions. In this election, at least, those who relied on the Internet appeared to be no better informed about politics in general than those who relied primarily on the press or on the radio.

Knowing Where the Parties Stand

Given that politics is usually a low priority in people's daily lives, it is perhaps understandable that Canadians are generally not that well informed about what is going on. A more reasonable criterion for judging knowledge levels may be the extent to which citizens know what they need to know in order to make an informed choice when an election comes along. One particularly pertinent piece of information is where the parties stand on the issues.

In the three most recent Canadian Election Studies, representative samples of Canadians have been asked to identify political parties with their issue positions. On only a handful of issues could even half of those interviewed get the answer correct (see Figure 3.3). During the 1993 federal election campaign, over a third of Canadians appeared to be unaware that the Conservatives were in favour of the Goods and Services Tax (GST), which had been introduced by the Conservatives under Prime Minister Brian Mulroney. Given its unpopularity, it is striking that more Canadians could not associate the GST with the Conservatives. A bare majority knew that the Liberals and/or the NDP were opposed to the GST. Similarly, right after the election, barely half seemed to know where those two parties stood on the recently negotiated North American Free Trade Agreement (NAFTA), despite the fact that both parties had campaigned hard against the original Canada-US Free Trade Agreement (CUFTA) in the 1988 election. In 1997 the only issue known to more than half of those interviewed after the election was the Reform Party's opposition to recognizing Quebec as a distinct society. And by the time the 2000 campaign was over, even the most widely known of the party stands appeared to be known to only two people in five.

Close to one-third of those interviewed in 2000 were unable to connect a single position with the right party, and another quarter were able to come up with only one correct answer. Only about 10 percent managed to associate more than three of the positions with the correct party. Such widespread ignorance of what the parties had been promising is a cause for concern in itself. However, it was not simply that large numbers of people were unable to answer. In the case of the NDP's promise to introduce a national prescription drug plan, almost as many people named the wrong party (22 percent) as named the NDP. And in the case of the Conservatives' promise to introduce a law requiring that the federal debt be repaid within twenty-five years, many more people named the wrong party (43 percent) than got the

Figure 3.3

Knowledge of party positions

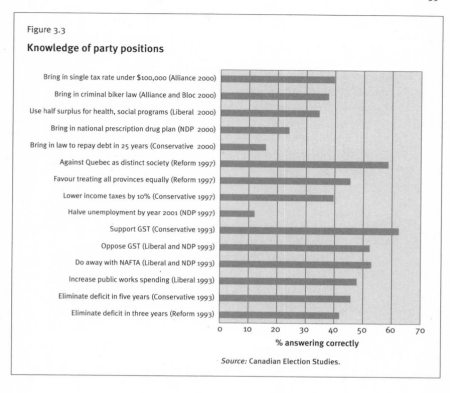

Source: Canadian Election Studies.

answer right (16 percent). Of course, some of these incorrect answers resulted from guessing (as did some of the correct answers), but some of them must also have reflected misinformation. Some people may well have ended up voting for the "wrong party" because they mistakenly thought that it shared their position on the issue in question.

Women would have been more likely than men to make this mistake (Figure 3.4). So would those who were poor or who had left school without a high school diploma. But even many of those who enjoyed the advantages of affluence and a university education hardly qualified as well informed about the parties' positions.

Young Canadians knew even less about the parties' positions than older Canadians. That finding cannot be explained away by the fact that young people had had shorter exposure to federal politics; the questions asked about the specific promises parties made going into

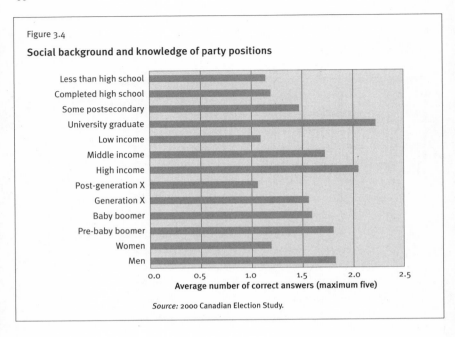

Figure 3.4

Social background and knowledge of party positions

Average number of correct answers (maximum five)

Source: 2000 Canadian Election Study.

the 2000 election. The same point applies to the lack of familiarity with the parties' positions on the part of people who had arrived in Canada within the previous ten years. Their low level of knowledge suggests that the process of adapting to a new setting does indeed hamper awareness of what is happening politically. Overall, though, it made little difference whether people were Canadian by birth or not.

Naturally, the more attention people paid to news about the election, the more they knew about the parties' positions by the time the election was over. The same was true of those who used the Internet to find out about the election (2.2 correct answers out of a possible 5, compared with a population average of 1.5 out of 5). Similarly, people who reported that they had often discussed the election with other people were much better informed (2.0) than those who had not talked about it at all (0.7). However, those who relied on family (0.6) or friends (0.7) as their primary source of information about the election were often unable to come up with a single correct answer. People who relied primarily on the press tended to be the most familiar with the parties' positions (1.8), followed by those who relied on the radio (1.6) or television (1.5). What is striking, though, is that even the most interested and attentive could typically come up with no more than two correct responses.

All of these findings drive home an important point. How much people know about politics is only partly a matter of their own motivation and abilities. The other side of the equation is the amount of effort that goes into the task of informing people. Viewed this way, it is hardly surprising that so few people in 1997 appeared to have heard about the NDP's promise to cut unemployment in half by the year 2001. After all, the party was effectively "off the radar screen" in that election (Nevitte et al. 2000, ch. 3). The NDP received no coverage in the news on one night in three during the 1997 election campaign. This visibility problem persisted in the 2000 election campaign. The NDP was the main focus in only 12 percent of the election stories broadcast on CBC and CTV during the campaign; it was never the focus of the lead story, and it featured in only 8 percent of the television news headlines about the campaign (Blais et al. 2002, ch. 2). The Conservative Party fared little better in the 2000 election. It was the main topic in 12 percent of the stories about the upcoming election and featured in 12 percent of the news headlines. Only 7 percent of the stories about the party appeared first in the nightly news. The two parties were even less visible on the French-language networks. Only an avid viewer of the news could have heard about the NDP's proposed prescription drug plan or the Conservatives' proposed law regarding the repayment of the federal debt.

Newspaper coverage was similarly uneven (Sampert and Trimble 2003). The NDP did not receive a single mention in the sixty-seven election headlines that ran on the front page of the *National Post* during the campaign, and was mentioned first in only 2 percent of the front-page stories in the *Globe and Mail.* Meanwhile, the Conservatives or their leader received first mention in just over 10 percent of the total front-page headlines in the *Post* and only 6 percent of the *Globe*'s front-page headlines.

Who Learns the Most during an Election?

So far, we have been looking at how much Canadians know about the parties' stands by the time an election is over. In principle at least, election campaigns provide voters with both the incentive and the opportunity to acquire the information they need to make an informed choice. Political parties have a strategic interest in informing voters of their stands on what they hope will prove to be winning issues and, for their part, voters have an incentive to learn what the parties have to say on the major issues of the day. Clearly, though, some Canadians learn more than others. The question is, how much do people learn from election campaigns? And is it those who know the least who learn the most?

One way to answer these questions is to divide citizens into groups based on their general knowledge of politics and then to see how much each group learns about the parties' issue stands over the course of the election campaign. It would be unrealistic to think that the "knowledge gap" could close over the brief span of an election campaign. We would expect those who are better informed about politics in general to be more knowledgeable about the parties' stands on the issues. Still, it is reasonable to suppose that the knowledge gap might narrow as the election draws near.

Data from the 1997 Canadian Election Study can be used to examine trends in the knowledge gap. During the campaign, people were asked which party was against recognizing Quebec as a distinct society (the Reform Party), which party was promising to lower personal income taxes by 10 percent (the Conservative Party), and which party was promising to cut unemployment in half by the year 2001 (the NDP). This enables us to create a simple campaign knowledge scale, based on the number of correct answers that each person gave. Our measure of people's general level of political knowledge is based on their ability to name their provincial premier, Canada's first female prime minister (Kim Campbell), Canada's finance minister (Paul Martin), and the president of the United States (Bill Clinton). These items were combined to create a general political knowledge scale.

Predictably, the level of general knowledge about politics changed little during the campaign. After all, neither the parties nor the media have any reason to promote general knowledge of politics during an election campaign, and voters have little incentive to acquire information that will not be of much use when it comes to deciding how to vote. The percentage of correct answers hovered at just over 50 percent throughout the campaign. Campaign knowledge, by contrast, did increase. The percentage of correct answers jumped from around 24 percent in the early days of the campaign to about 33 percent by the campaign's close. In relative terms, this amounts to an increase of almost 40 percent. When political information is sufficiently available and, more importantly, pertinent, some voters do apparently acquire factual information that may help to make their choices more informed.

So learning clearly does take place during an election campaign. The key question, then, is *who* learns. Are people who are less informed about politics in general able to close the knowledge gap when they need to? To answer this question, we tracked the gap in campaign knowledge between those who were fairly well informed about politics in general and those who were not. The first group consisted of people who got at least three of the four general political knowledge questions right (48 percent), while the second group was made up of people who got none or only one right (23 percent).

It turns out that the gap in knowledge of the parties' campaign promises actually widened during the election campaign. At the beginning of the 1997 campaign, the gap was around 20 points. Among those who were generally well informed about politics, the percentage of correct answers was about 35 percent, compared with only 15 percent among the poorly informed. By the end of the campaign, the gap had grown to around 28 points, because knowledge levels had risen to 45 percent among those who were well informed about politics in general but barely moved among those who were not. The well informed used the opportunity to become even better informed, while those who were poorly informed appeared to acquire little new information. The overall gains in information were clearly more pronounced among those who were better informed about politics to begin with. Thus, it is older, well-educated men who typically learn the most during a campaign. Meanwhile, those who need to learn the most seem to learn the least.

Matthew Mendelsohn and Fred Cutler (2000) found a similar pattern in their analysis of how much Canadians learned about positions on the Charlottetown Accord over the course of the 1992 referendum campaign. People did learn as the campaign progressed, but the knowledge gains were very modest. And the campaign most certainly did not "transform an otherwise poorly informed citizenry into a community of political junkies" (p. 689). More importantly, those who were generally poorly informed tended to make only modest gains, and those gains typically occurred later in the campaign. In contrast to the 1997 federal election campaign, though, the best informed did not seem to learn much at all from the campaign. This probably reflected a "ceiling effect"; people who were generally well informed about politics typically knew from the outset where prominent figures like former prime minister Pierre Trudeau stood, and so there was little for them to learn. The most learning took place in the next-best informed group. The fact that the least informed made only small gains in knowledge casts doubt on the optimistic assumption that referendums provide an "instrument of civic education" (Barber 1984, 284).

These findings raise a large question: who – or what – is to blame if the knowledge gap fails to narrow even when citizens have a political choice to make? Perhaps Canadians are just apathetic citizens who know little and care less. Certainly, having prior knowledge seems to help people both make sense of new information and recall it (Price and Hsu 1992). People who are knowledgeable about politics may have well-developed "partisan schemas" that enable them to comprehend and to integrate new pieces of information (Rhee and Cappella 1997). For example, someone reasonably familiar with politics in Canada might already know that the NDP is the party that favours public provision, and from that prior knowledge they might infer that the NDP's response to the high cost of prescription drugs would be to propose a national prescription drug plan. Apathy is also a factor. Predictably, the people with the least interest in the campaign learn the least because they pay little or no attention to news about the election on television. However, ignorance and apathy are only part of the story. The knowledge gap phenomenon is also a function of campaigns that do little to inform. This becomes clear when we examine how the availability of information in the media affects the campaign knowledge gap.

Election campaigns can be thought of as struggles for control of the agenda, with each party vying to draw voters' attention to its stands on the issues. The media are critical players in this competition to control the election agenda. Even in the Internet age, political parties are still heavily dependent on the media for getting their messages across to voters. The media, however, are not simply a neutral transmission belt between the parties and the electorate. In a very literal sense, they mediate communication flows. This mediating role involves highlighting some messages and downplaying others. As a result, some issues are widely covered, some receive only modest coverage, and some are more or less ignored altogether (Blais et al. 2002, ch. 2). This variation in coverage enables us to illustrate how the knowledge gap on particular issues in 1997 was affected by the amount of coverage those issues received in the media.

A content analysis of the late evening newscasts on the four main English- and French-language television networks, two public (CBC and SRC) and two private (CTV and TVA), revealed that the nightly media coverage of the 1997 campaign was dominated by news about the electoral race (the leaders' tours, polls, strategies, campaign ads, and so on). Three-quarters of the news items on both the English and French networks featured some aspect or another of the race. This focus on the "horse race" is typical of the patterns of media coverage found in most Canadian elections and indeed in Western democracies generally (Mendelsohn 1993; Norris et al. 1999). The issues took second place, but the relevant consideration here is how much coverage was given to each of the three issues that we have been examining. The Reform Party's position on recognizing Quebec as a distinct society received the most coverage, and that coverage increased as the campaign progressed. The NDP's policy on jobs, by contrast, received relatively little coverage, especially in the latter part of the campaign.

Coverage of the Conservatives' position on tax cuts, meanwhile, fell between these two extremes. The results for the four networks revealed broadly similar patterns.

The intensity of media coverage clearly affected the size and evolution of the gaps in campaign knowledge. When an issue receives a good deal of coverage, even those who are generally poorly informed about politics may learn of a party's stand. This was the case for Reform's opposition to recognizing Quebec as a distinct society. Coverage was sufficiently intense that even some people who were typically poorly informed about politics got to hear about it. By the end of the campaign, 23 percent of them knew of the promise, compared with just 14 percent at the beginning. A similar gain in knowledge was apparent among the well informed, however, and so the knowledge gap remained at about 60 points.

Conversely, even people who are generally well informed about politics may fail to learn much if a party's stand does not make the news. This was the case for the NDP's commitment to cutting unemployment. Only 15 percent of the relatively well informed identified the NDP as the party making this promise. People who were poorly informed did even worse (10 percent). This gap barely changed over the course of the campaign. Apparently, coverage of the unemployment issue was too limited for even the well informed to pick up on the NDP promise.

In the case of the Conservative promise to cut taxes, by contrast, the knowledge gap substantially increased during the campaign, widening from about 17 points at the beginning of the campaign to 40 points at the close. The moderate amount of media coverage given to the taxation issues was enough, apparently, to attract the attention of those who were generally well informed about politics, but not enough to reach those who were less attentive.

Unless an issue receives intense media coverage, then, campaign learning will mostly be confined to those who are generally well informed about politics. The implication is clear. When the media put a particular issue under the spotlight, some people who do not normally pay much attention to politics may get to know where a party stands. Even relatively intense media coverage may not be enough to close the knowledge gap (or even narrow it), as the case of the Reform stance on Quebec underlines. Still, the essential point is that the extent to which the media focus on the issues affects the potential for campaign learning.

And campaign learning matters. When voters discover where a given party stands on a particular issue, they have an additional piece of information to consider when making their vote choice. That vote choice could well change if voters were previously unaware of the party's stand or if they had erroneously thought that some other party was closer to them on the issue. Imagine a voter in the 1997 election who wanted tax cuts but who was unaware that the Conservatives were promising to cut taxes by 10 percent. Campaign learning presents citizens with an opportunity to bring their vote choice in line with their true preferences.

Can Canadians Tell Left from Right?

Canadians' factual knowledge of politics is one thing, but there is another, more sophisticated type of knowledge that citizens need in order to participate meaningfully in the country's political life. What we might call "conceptual knowledge" entails an understanding of political concepts like "left" and "right." Conceptual knowledge may seem unduly abstract, but we need only to glance through a newspaper or turn on the television news to see just how frequently these kinds of terms are used. Since the collapse of the Progressive Conservative Party in 1993, media commentary has debated the prospects for "uniting the right." Similarly, the NDP's electoral woes have prompted discussions of the "future of the left" in Canada. But just how many Canadians actually understand what the terms "left" and "right" mean?

In fact, many Canadians have either a shaky grasp or no grasp at all of this basic ideological terminology. As part of the 1984 Canadian Election Study, Ronald Lambert and his colleagues (1986) set out to discover what the terms "left" and "right" meant to Canadians. At that time, only 40 percent of the sample could — or would — define the terms. And many of those who did venture definitions seemed to have quite fuzzy understandings. For example, some people equated "right" with being in the right, and they came up with synonyms like "principled" or "honest."

In the 1980s, references to the left or to the right figured much less prominently in news reports and in political debate. However, more frequent and explicit use of this terminology does not seem to have enhanced Canadians' conceptual knowledge very much. The 2000 Canadian Election Study asked Canadians to identify whether each of the federal parties was on the left, on the right, or in the centre. Barely a third of the sample correctly identified the NDP as being on the left. Fully half of those interviewed were either unsure how to place the party (31 percent) or else admitted that they did not understand what the terms meant (19 percent). Similarly, only a third placed the Alliance on the right.

Given what we know about factual knowledge, it comes as no surprise that women had a harder time with these questions than men. Only 23 percent of women placed the NDP correctly, compared with 40 percent of men. The figures were almost identical for the Alliance: 24 percent of women put the party on the right, compared with 42 percent of men. Young Canadians were also less likely to place the two parties correctly. Only 18 percent identified the NDP as being on the left, while 24 percent put the Alliance on the right. These figures rose to 39 percent and 36 percent, respectively, among older Canadians.

People's income level and educational background both made a huge difference. Among poor Canadians, fewer than one in five could correctly locate the NDP on the left or the Alliance on the right. Wealthy Canadians did much better: more than one in two placed the NDP correctly and almost as many did the same for the Alliance. Similar gaps separated university graduates from those who left school without a high school diploma. The pattern is now familiar: affluence did not compensate for lack of schooling, and higher education did not make up for straitened financial circumstances. The income gaps persisted at every level of schooling, just as the education gaps persisted regardless of household income. But even many of the most advantaged Canadians have difficulty locating the parties correctly: fewer than three in four wealthy, university-educated Canadians were able to place the two parties that anchor the opposite ends of the left-right spectrum in Canada.

Discussion

The Canadian public contains deep pockets of political ignorance and political illiteracy. Over 40 percent of Canadians were unable to name the leaders of the federal political parties, even though they were being interviewed right after an election in which those leaders had figured prominently. As for the parties' issue positions, 30 percent of Canadians could not identify one single promise with the party making it. And most Canadians were unable to identify which party was on the left and which was on the right. Disturbing as these figures are, they probably overstate the level of political knowledge in the country for the simple reason that people who tune out politics altogether are less likely to agree to take part in an election survey.

The social differences in the distribution of political knowledge are also cause for concern. Women typically know less than men, the young know less than older Canadians, and the poor know less than the wealthy. Although education enhances knowledge about politics, it does not close these knowledge gaps. And far from having an equalizing effect, election campaigns can actually end up widening these knowledge gaps. It is worth noting, though, that intense media coverage can help even the poorly informed to learn more about a party's stance.

These findings are not unique to Canada. Decades of study of information levels in the United States have led many to conclude that "the mean level is very low but the variance is very high" (Converse 2000, 331). Like the average Canadian, the average American knows rather little about politics, but there are Americans, as there are Canadians, who know a great deal. The US verdict is also similar when it comes to conceptual knowledge: most American voters lack a grasp of basic ideological terminology (Converse 1990).

What are the implications of these findings for the responsiveness of democratic politics in Canada? The knowledge gap is not a peculiarly political phenomenon. Communication scholars were the first to observe the phenomenon in the context of information campaigns, and they, too, emphasized the uneven diffusion of information across social groups (Tichenor, Donohue, and Olien 1970; Gaziano and Gaziano 1996; Viswanath and Finnegan 1996; Kwak 1999). They recognized early on that "relative deprivation of knowledge may lead to a relative deprivation of power" (Donohue, Tichenor, and Olien 1973, 4). As Viswanath and Finnegan argue, "knowledge inequalities ... may lead to serious power differentials and reflect on the capacity of [social systems] to serve the needs of all their members equitably" (p. 189).

The findings presented in this chapter raise questions about both the effectiveness of election campaigns and the democratic quality of the electoral process. In theory, election campaigns provide unique opportunities to "lift the bottom" (Delli Carpini and Keeter 1996, 280, 287). In reality, though, election campaigns in Canada and elsewhere rarely prove to be significant educational experiences (Butler and Kavanagh, 1997). Parties are out to win votes and the media are out to win ratings. Whether courting voters or wooing viewers, it is not clear that these efforts help citizens to make enlightened choices.

CHAPTER 3

- Significant numbers of Canadians do not know such simple facts as the names of the federal party leaders, the federal finance minister, or even their prime minister or premier.

- Even more Canadians are unaware of where the political parties stand on some of the issues of the day.

- Women, poorer Canadians, the young, and those with less formal schooling typically know less about politics.

- Election campaigns may cause the knowledge gaps to widen, unless there is intense media coverage of a party's position.

- Many Canadians are unfamiliar with basic ideological terminology and have problems placing even ideologically distinctive parties on the left-right spectrum.

4 CAN CANADIANS GET BY WITH LESS INFORMATION?

Many Canadians' knowledge of politics may be sketchy, but does this necessarily mean that they get it "wrong" when translating their preferences into an appropriate political choice? Two bodies of literature seem to provide grounds for optimism. The low-information rationality argument points to a variety of information shortcuts that can help people arrive at the same choices they would make if they were fully informed (Popkin 1991; Sniderman, Brody, and Tetlock 1991). By relying on these shortcuts, people can "be knowledgeable in their reasoning about political choices without necessarily possessing a large body of knowledge about politics" (Sniderman, Brody, and Tetlock 1991, 19). Meanwhile, the aggregationist thesis suggests that *collective* public opinion can accurately reflect the collective interests and values of the citizenry, even though many *individual* expressions of opinion are inconsistent and ill informed (Page and Shapiro 1992).

In this chapter, we examine whether the use of information shortcuts and aggregation really do compensate for shortfalls in information. Who benefits the most from information shortcuts? Is it the poorly informed? Or do information shortcuts mainly help the well informed make better use of their store of knowledge? Would collective opinion really look much as it does now if Canadians were better informed about politics? Does collective opinion reflect the interests of some social groups better than others? And, finally, what if some Canadians are not simply *un*informed, but *mis*informed? How many Canadians get basic policy-relevant facts wrong? Who is most susceptible to misinformation? And does misinformation matter?

Do Information Shortcuts Compensate for Shortfalls in Information?

According to the low-information rationality argument, citizens can make up for their lack of information about politics by relying on information shortcuts, or heuristics. Many citizens may be ill acquainted with the facts, but they can get by without them by drawing on a variety of readily available cues. According to Samuel Popkin (1991, 44), "At the heart of gut rationality are information shortcuts – easily obtained and used forms of information that serve as 'second-best' substitutes for harder-to-obtain kinds of data. Shortcuts that voters use incorporate learning from past experiences, daily life, the media, and political campaigns."

All sorts of information shortcuts have been suggested. For example, people can take cues from people who are more knowledgeable and who can be counted upon to share the same needs and values. This can be as simple as heeding the advice of a friend or neighbour who happens to know more. Imagine a person who is not very well informed about the workings of the health care system, but has a friend or neighbour who is a health care worker. It would make sense to listen to what that person has to say about the implications of charging user fees for visits to the doctor's office or allowing private hospitals to be set up in Canada.

The advice does not have to come from a friend or neighbour. People can also look at who is advocating and who is opposing a particular policy change. It may be enough for them to ask themselves how they feel about the party or politician that is taking the initiative on the issue (the "agenda-setter"). The 1988 federal election provides a prime example of the use of this sort of shortcut. The election was a virtual referendum on the Canada-US Free Trade Agreement. CUFTA was a complex issue if ever there was one, but for some poorly informed voters the vote decision was hugely simplified by the opposition parties' rhetorical ploy of linking the agreement to the Conservative prime minister, Brian Mulroney (see Johnston et al. 1992). Poorly informed voters could simply use their feelings about Mulroney as a guide.

Voters may also be able to get some clues about which side to take by consulting their feelings about the people or organizations that intervene publicly in the debate ("intervenors"). Arthur Lupia (1994) gives a good example of this. When California voters had to decide on a series of proposals on automobile insurance, voters who knew little about the proposals were able to mimic the choices of the well informed simply by knowing where the insurance industry stood on each proposal. In the case of the 1988 Canadian election, important interventions were made by groups like the Business Council on National Issues, the Canadian Automobile Workers' Union, and the National Action Committee on the Status of Women. Provided voters knew what position the organization in question had taken on CUFTA, they could simply ask themselves how they felt about big business, unions, or the women's movement and support or oppose CUFTA accordingly.

Partisanship can also serve as a handy information shortcut. A person who is a staunch Liberal, say, can just follow the Liberal lead on a given issue without investing the time and energy required to become informed about either the issue itself or the views of competing parties. This makes sense as a cost-saving strategy so long as that person is keeping an eye on the party's performance to be sure that it is not deviating from its basic course (Jenson 1976, 31).

Meanwhile, candidates can be evaluated on the basis of their perceived personality traits or on their conduct of the campaign. Something as simple as a politician's social background characteristics can serve as a basis for inferring where she or he stands on the issues (Popkin 1991). For example, Monika McDermott (1997, 1998) has shown how voters in low-information elections in the United States can use the candidates' race and gender to estimate their ideological stances, provided they know that female and Afro-American politicians are typically more liberal than their white male counterparts. Then there is "the simplest shortcut of all," namely, "the degree of obvious demographic similarity" between the voter and the candidate (Cutler 2002, 467). Fred Cutler found that, net of other influences, Canadians are more likely to vote for a party whose leader is of the same sex, comes from the same region, and belongs to the same linguistic group. It is not unreasonable to think that a candidate who comes from a similar social background will be more likely to understand the voter's needs and wants (Johnston et al. 1992, 169).

When it comes to deciding how to vote, Morris Fiorina (1993) has shown that people can simplify their choice by focusing on how well or poorly the incumbent party has performed. The economic voting model, for example, assumes a simple "reward-and-punish" calculus: vote to re-elect the incumbent in good economic times, and throw the incumbent out in bad times. In its simplest form, all voters have to do is to consult their own pocketbooks and ask themselves whether they are better or worse off since the incumbent was elected.

However, Paul Sniderman and his colleagues (1991, 28) have cautioned against the proliferation of shortcuts: "As with scalpels, the notion of heuristics works best if used sparingly." They focus on the role of affect, or how people feel toward politically salient groups. They argue that affect-driven reasoning holds the key to resolving "a deep puzzle," namely, "If ordinary people know and understand so little about politics, how can it be possible that they frequently figure out what they are for and against politically?" (p. 15). Their answer to this question is that people can compensate for their shortfalls in political information by relying on their group likes and dislikes: "A person is not required to be acquainted with the particular details of a specific policy to figure out whether he or she is for or against it. It suffices to know that a policy aims to help or hurt [a particular group]: People may then support or oppose it, consistently and coherently, simply according to whether they are hostile or sympathetic [to that group]" (p. 22). Imagine a proposal to oblige people who are on welfare to accept any job that is offered to them, or else lose their benefits. All people would need to do to decide where they stand on this is to ask themselves how they feel about people on welfare. If they feel negative, they will support the proposal; if they feel positive, they will oppose it. In either case, they are spared the need to invest effort in learning more about the specifics of the proposal.

The low-information rationality argument certainly has its share of critics. Kuklinski and his colleagues (Kuklinski and Hurley 1994; Kuklinski and Quirk 2000), in particular, have suggested that information shortcuts, or heuristics, can lead to inferior decisions. In cognitive psychology, reliance on heuristics is typically considered to be "automatic, unconscious, and frequently dysfunctional" (Kuklinski and Quirk 2000, 166). When people rely on cues and other heuristics, they are processing information peripherally rather than centrally, and this means that they typically expend little cognitive energy in assessing the validity of the information itself. This is why Kuklinski and Hurley (1994, 732) argue that, "Like religion, taking political cues may be a matter of faith," especially given the lack of feedback mechanisms that would enable people to tell whether their information shortcuts have led to the right choice or not.

It is important to remember that information shortcuts were not posited as a crutch for people who are tuning out of politics altogether. As Delli Carpini and Keeter (1996, 52) point out, "The heuristic model is based on *low* information rationality, not *no* information rationality." In Popkin's (1991) formulation, for example, low-information rationality combines politically relevant information acquired in the course of everyday life with information gleaned from the media and from political campaigns. So most information shortcuts presuppose a fair amount of political information. Taking cues from "agenda-setters" or from "intervenors," for example, requires sufficient political awareness to know who is making the proposal and who else has been making public pronouncements on the subject. Similarly, voters need to know what the government has been doing in order to apply the reward-and-punish calculus. Some shortcuts presuppose more information than others. A candidate's gender and race may be self-evident, but other characteristics, like religion, are not, which probably explains why Cutler (2002) found that Canadians did not seem to use a party leader's religious affiliation as a cue. Meanwhile, if voters are going to use a candidate's gender, say, to make inferences about her ideological orientations, they have to know that women tend to be more liberal than men.

In each of these examples, people can only use the cue appropriately if they possess some contextual information about politics. Low-information rationality is all about using shortcuts to enable people to go beyond the information *they already have.* This is why the use of shortcuts is not confined to poorly informed voters. On the contrary, even voters who are well informed rely on shortcuts for the simple reason that being well informed is not the same thing as being fully informed. Cutler (2002) found that well-informed voters were just as likely as poorly informed voters to use "the simplest shortcut of all." Where the well informed differ is in the extent of their reliance on shortcuts (as opposed to other factors) and in the sort of shortcuts they use (Sniderman, Brody, and Tetlock 1991; Johnston et al. 1996). Ideology is a prime example of a shortcut that is used most heavily by the best informed. However, feelings are not irrelevant to the political reasoning of the well informed. What information, or political sophistication more generally, does is influence the way that feelings are used in reasoning about politics.

Information shortcuts do not necessarily make for enlightened choices (Bartels 1996; Kuklinski and Quirk 2000; Kuklinski and Hurley 1994). Indeed, their use could result in systematic biases. Assuming that a female politician is liberal simply because she is a woman, for example, could lead a voter seriously astray. Women politicians may *tend* to be more liberal than their male counterparts, but many women are at the conservative end of the ideological spectrum. Meanwhile, judgments based on group likes and dislikes may be distorted by feelings that are based on little more than crude and inaccurate stereotypes that stubbornly resist correction. And there is the risk of succumbing to a "false-consensus effect" whereby people mistakenly assume that the opinions of people they like are similar to their own

(Sniderman, Brody, and Tetlock 1991). The point, once again, is that people can make proper use of shortcuts only if they know something about politics to begin with.

As for economic voting, it may *seem* rational enough: reward the incumbent for good economic performance and punish the incumbent for poor performance. However, this assumes that the incumbent is actually responsible for the performance of the economy. To the extent that the performance of the economy is beyond the incumbent's control, voting on the basis of economic performance "for the most part ... merely rewards good economic luck and punishes bad" (Kuklinski and Quirk 2000, 158). And voting on the basis of economic performance can create perverse incentives for incumbent governments to focus on the short term.

Taking cues from public figures can sometimes be problematic, too. Kuklinski and Hurley (1994), for example, have shown how a politician's race can obscure more relevant information, such as the politician's ideological orientation or prior policy stands. Voters need to be on their guard. Individuals and organizations intervene in public debates because they want to influence public opinion. In doing so, they may resort to rhetorical ploys and maybe even outright manipulation. This is one reason that Kuklinski and Quirk (2000, 168) are skeptical of cue-taking: "Politicians are not in the business of educating the public. Instead, they use rhetoric to trigger the psychological mechanisms that distort judgment – presenting isolated, unrepresentative facts and seeking to evoke an emotional response rather than encourage rational deliberation." This behaviour is not limited to politicians.

A study of voting in the 1992 referendum on the Charlottetown Accord illustrates some of the difficulties with the low-information rationality thesis, and also provides insight into how information – or lack thereof – affects political choices. Canadians were being asked to vote on a complex and comprehensive package of constitutional proposals that was intended to bring Quebec into the constitution (Johnston et al. 1996; Blais et al. 1996). The referendum campaign featured a highly publicized intervention by former prime minister Pierre Trudeau. Within days of his speech urging rejection of the Accord, the "yes" vote dropped by 20 points outside Quebec. This seems like prima facie evidence in support of the importance of interventions. But rather than serving as an information shortcut for poorly informed voters, the various interventions seemed to "make the cognitively rich richer" (Johnston et al. 1996, 283). Interventions can only help the poorly informed if the latter are actually aware of them. But awareness of campaign interventions was "very spotty and imperfect" (Johnston et al. 1996, 282): the people who needed interventions the most were the least likely to know about them. Even at the end of the campaign, almost one-third of voters (30 percent) failed to locate Trudeau correctly among the opponents of the Accord. The figure was similar for former Reform Party leader Preston Manning, who also came out firmly in opposition. Outside Quebec, nearly half the voters were aware of only two interventions, or fewer. In Quebec, the figure rose to close to three-fifths.

On the other hand, low-information voters were the most affected by a barrage of negative polls late in the campaign. Their support dropped when polls showed that the Accord was likely to fail. Far from bringing their vote closer into line with that of high-information voters, however, this polling information actually caused them to diverge even further. Voters who were already well informed simply did not need the additional information. They had already mostly made their minds up based on other considerations.

Just as Sniderman and his colleagues (1991) argued, well-informed voters and poorly informed voters alike relied on their feelings. In fact, in Quebec, feelings about Canada carried the most weight with the well informed, and outside Quebec, feelings about the province were as important to well-informed voters as they were to those who knew rather little. Where the well informed differed was in bringing more abstract ideas to bear on their vote choice as well. For example, conceptions of Canada and orientations toward minorities affected the votes only of the well informed.

Indeed, the well informed arrived at their vote choice through reasoning chains that were both complex and hierarchical. Among high-information voters, abstract ideas and group sentiment affected evaluations of intervenors and agenda-setters, which, in turn, influenced substantive considerations about the Accord. Among low-information voters, by contrast, the causal arrow typically ran straight from feelings to vote choice. This is why "feelings do not make up for ideas, and poorly informed voters make much less consistent choices than well-informed voters do" (Johnston et al. 1996, 282). Poorly informed voters were much less likely than well informed voters to take positions on either the specific provisions of the constitutional accord or the general arguments that were advanced in its support. And when they did take a position, they were much less likely to translate that position into the "correct" vote choice. Indeed, relative to their opinions about the specific elements of the Accord and its supporting arguments, their vote appeared to be more or less random.

Information shortcuts can help some voters to arrive at the right choice, but "'low-information' rationality is not the great equalizer for the expression of preferences in democracies" (Cutler 2002, 484). Low-information rationality assumes that people have at least a modicum of information about politics. This is why people who are most in need of information shortcuts are often the least likely to be able to make use of them (Johnston et al. 1996). Even the "simplest shortcut of all" will be of little help to people who tune out of politics so completely that they do not know who the party leaders are.

Does Aggregation Compensate for Shortfalls in Information?

The aggregationist argument assumes that people like this will express more or less random opinions on most issues. Because they know little about politics and care less, their opinions will fluctuate in unpredictable ways. The very fact that their opinions are random, though, means that they will cancel one another out in the process of aggregation and we will be left with the nonrandom opinions of the well informed.

The aggregationist argument is based on the Condorcet jury theorem, which shows that, under certain conditions, the quality of group decisions can be much higher than the quality of the decisions of the individuals that comprise the group. Applied to questions of political choice, this theorem shows that if each voter has a better than 50-50 chance of making the "right choice," the probability of the majority choice being "right" is virtually 100 percent. In this context, the "right choice" means the choice that voters would make if they were fully informed. The probability of an individual voter getting it right need only be very slightly higher than 50 percent for this result to occur.

Page and Shapiro (1992) argue that information shortcuts help ensure that this condition is met. In support of their argument, they are able to show that US public opinion is stable and coherent and that it moves in predictable ways in response to changing conditions and new information. However, the fact that collective public opinion reacts to changing circumstances in understandable ways does not necessarily qualify it as rational. As Kuklinski and Quirk (2000, 161) note, "Collective opinion could favor unrealistically low taxes and yet still respond to the budget deficit; it could favor excessively harsh criminal sentences and still respond to crime rates; favor a defense budget twice as large as needed and still vary with level of international tension, etc." In other words, individual and collective opinions alike are subject not just to random error but to systematic biases and distortion.

From the perspective of inclusiveness and responsiveness, though, the aggregationist argument has a more critical flaw: it overlooks the fact that there are systematic *social* biases in the distribution of political knowledge (Althaus 1998). As we have seen, it is not simply that some citizens know more about politics than others; it is that some *categories* of citizen typically know more than others. Older, affluent, educated, white men tend to be the best informed about politics, and their interests and values will thus be disproportionately reflected in any expression of collective preferences. People who are poorly informed are less likely to form opinions that are consistent with their interests and values, and so the probability of their making the "right choice" may well fall below 51 percent.

Althaus (1998) has demonstrated that the distribution of US public opinion on many policy issues would look quite different if the least informed citizens were as well informed about politics as the best informed: "The uneven social distribution of political knowledge causes the mass public consistently to appear more progressive on some issues and more conservative on others than might be the case if all citizens were equally informed about politics" (p. 545). Is this true of Canadian public opinion as well? To answer this question, we have simulated what the distribution of opinion on various questions from the 2000 Canadian Election Study would look like if all Canadians were equally well informed about politics. The simulations involve assigning the preferences (as estimated by a regression model) of the most informed members of a given social group to all members of that group (see Althaus 1998).

For the twenty-six questions examined, the average difference between actual and informed opinion was almost 5.5 percentage points. For questions of social policy, such as immigration, the death penalty, gay marriage, and the status of women and racial minorities, the average difference was almost 7.5 points. Meanwhile, questions dealing with fiscal policy and with the role of the state versus the market had an average difference of just over 4 percentage points. On a number of questions only small differences were registered, suggesting that aggregation *can* compensate for shortfalls in information. However, on the ten questions that changed by more than 5 points, informed opinion differed from actual opinion by an average of almost 10 points (see Figure 4.1). This is similar to the pattern observed by Althaus: "When collective opinion changed by more than a few points, it tended to shift quite dramatically" (1998, 551). The largest changes occurred for opinions about immigration (15.0 points), the power of business (12.8 points), the death penalty (11.9 points), and abortion (11.0 points).

Figure 4.1

Actual versus "informed" opinion

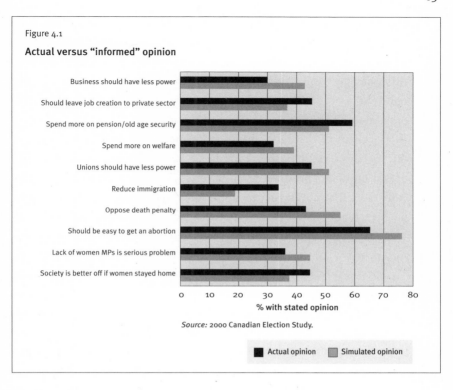

Business should have less power

Should leave job creation to private sector

Spend more on pension/old age security

Spend more on welfare

Unions should have less power

Reduce immigration

Oppose death penalty

Should be easy to get an abortion

Lack of women MPs is serious problem

Society is better off if women stayed home

% with stated opinion

Source: 2000 Canadian Election Study.

■ Actual opinion   ▨ Simulated opinion

Simply looking at the magnitude of the difference between actual and informed opinion can be misleading. A change from 45 percent support to 55 percent support for a given policy direction is more consequential than a change from 75 percent to 85 percent. The latter merely reinforces the majority opinion, whereas the former actually represents a change in the direction of that opinion. A good way to get a sense of the significance of the shifts we observed is to ask how often the collective preference changed from a majority (or minority) in favour to either a tie (defined as being within three points either way of a 50-50 split) or else a majority (or minority) opposed (Althaus 1998). According to this criterion, the collective preference on five of the twenty-six questions changed when we simulated informed preferences. (Note that our standard for "informed opinion" was not particularly high. It required familiarity with only the names of the federal party leaders and the promises made by their parties in the 2000 federal election.) The most dramatic change occurred on the death penalty, where opinion went from 43 percent opposed to 55 percent opposed. Interestingly, when MPs in Ottawa last debated the death penalty, opinion moved in a liberal direction as the debate evolved and as MPs presumably became better informed about the issue.

As critics of the aggregationist argument would predict, when it differs, informed opinion tends to be *systematically* different from actual opinion. Informed opinion on social policy questions is typically more liberal than actual opinion. It is more opposed to the death penalty, more likely to think that abortions should be easy to obtain, and more concerned about the lack of women MPs, and it is less likely to favour traditional gender roles or reductions in immigration (see Figure 4.1). Informed opinion is also more supportive of gay marriage and of "doing more" for racial minorities. There are only two exceptions: informed opinion is more ambivalent about gun control and a little less concerned about the lack of visible minority MPs. It is important to emphasize that the simulations controlled for education. University graduates tend to be more liberal on questions of social policy, and they also tend to be better informed, but this does not explain why information leads to more liberal positions.

Informed opinion also tends to be more liberal on fiscal questions and questions about the role of the state versus the market, but the tendency is weaker. It applies to ten of the sixteen questions, including the power of business, the role of government in job creation, and spending on welfare (see Figure 4.1), as well as cutting funding to provinces that impose user fees and doing more to reduce the gap between rich and poor. Notable exceptions include spending on pensions and old age security and the power of unions. In both cases, informed opinion is evenly divided where actual opinion has a more liberal bent.

The limitations of the aggregationist argument become clear when we compare the effects of our simulations on various social groups. The differences between actual opinion and informed opinion are consistently larger for some social groups than for others (see Figure 4.2).

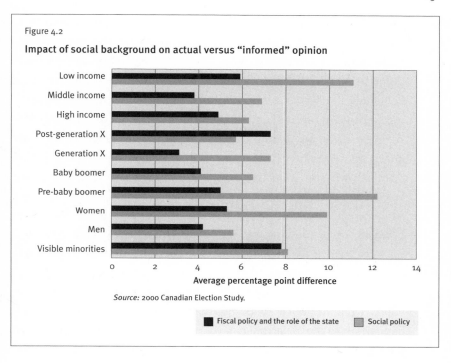

Figure 4.2

Impact of social background on actual versus "informed" opinion

Average percentage point difference

Source: 2000 Canadian Election Study.

■ Fiscal policy and the role of the state   ▓ Social policy

This is a reflection of the socially uneven distribution of political information. When it comes to social questions, the collective opinions of older Canadians, less affluent Canadians, women, and members of visible minorities, would all likely differ if they were better informed. The same is true of young Canadians and visible minorities when it comes to questions of fiscal policy and the role of the state.

On almost every question of social policy, the informed opinion of Canadians born before 1945 is more liberal than actual opinion. Some of the differences are quite dramatic. If older Canadians were better informed, opposition to the death penalty could increase by over 20 points in this age group, changing a minority opinion to a clear majority opposed. The same is true of views about the lack of women MPs in the House of Commons. Meanwhile, their support for reducing immigration would drop by close to 20 points. The sole exception to this pattern is views about gun control, which might actually be less favourable if older Canadians were all well informed. While the differences between actual and informed opinion are generally more muted on questions of fiscal policy and the role of the state, the pattern is the same: opinions would be more liberal if information levels were higher. There are only two exceptions: views about defence cuts would not change, and fewer older Canadians would favour increased spending on pensions and old age security. Overall, collective opinion in this segment of the population would shift by more than 10 points on six questions and by over 5 points on another eleven.

Meanwhile, the collective opinions of young Canadians would shift by over 10 points on six questions and over 5 points on a further eight. In contrast to older Canadians, though, the largest differences between actual and informed opinion in this age group were recorded for questions of fiscal policy and the role of the state. And informed opinion was more liberal on some questions, but more conservative on others. For example, if young Canadians were better informed, their support for increased spending on welfare would rise by 13 points, opposition to the government's role in job creation would drop by 20 points, and support for reducing the power of business would increase by 20 points. At the same time, though, support for reducing the power of unions would also increase by about 17 points.

Simulating the opinions of an informed electorate has a much more consistent effect for women. On questions of social policy, informed opinion has quite a marked liberal bent. If they were better informed, women would be less likely to favour cuts in immigration (18 points), and they would be more likely to reject traditional conceptions of gender roles (13 points), to oppose the death penalty (13 points) and to think that abortions should be easy to obtain (16 points). There are only two exceptions to this pattern: informed opinion is less likely to be concerned about the lack of minority MPs (5 points) or to favour gun control (7 points). The differences between actual and informed opinion on questions of fiscal policy and the role of the state versus the market are generally less sharp, with the notable exception of views about free enterprise. If they were better informed, more women would favour reducing the power of business (20 points) and fewer would want job creation left to the private sector (11 points). Their support for increased spending on welfare would rise (10 points), but so would their desire to see unions have less power (8 points).

The differences between actual and informed opinion are greater for women than for men. This is only to be expected, since women typically know less about political affairs than men. But if women were as well informed as men, the opinions of men and women would typically differ more than they do, not less. The gap would widen by more than 10 points on four questions and by more than 5 points on another six questions. These include opinions about user fees for visits to the doctor, defence spending, gender roles, and the power of business. This drives home an important point. The needs and wants of different social groups are not the same, but as long as some groups are consistently less informed than others, collective expressions of opinion may fail to reflect these differences. When this happens, public policy may be less responsive to those needs and wants.

An informed electorate does not necessarily mean deeper divisions in public opinion. The gap between rich and poor increased on three questions by over 10 points and on another seven by over 5 points, but it narrowed on another six questions. Among low-income Canadians, more information would mean less support for cuts in immigration (21 points), greater opposition to the death penalty (14 points), and more support for abortion (15 points). In each case, this would bring them closer to the views of affluent Canadians. However, the gap would widen on gun control by up to 18 points, as support for gun control would drop among poorer Canadians and increase among the affluent.

A gap would also open up on questions relating to free enterprise. Among rich and poor alike, informed opinion is more liberal, but information makes more difference to the poor than the rich. Poorer Canadians would be much less likely to want job creation left entirely to the private sector (16 points) or to want business to have as much power (19 points). Their opposition to the creation of private hospitals would increase (7 points), and they would want more done to reduce the gap between rich and poor (7 points) and more spent on welfare (5 points).

Among the poor, actual and informed opinion differed by more than 10 points on eight questions and by more than 5 points on another eight.

The same was true of visible minorities, but again the effects of information were not very consistent. Informed opinion was more liberal on gay marriage (23 points), the power of business (16 points), and job creation (15 points), but less liberal on pensions and old age security (16 points), employment insurance (9 points), user fees for visits to the doctor (8 points), and funding for provinces that allow user fees (9 points). Interestingly, informed opinion was also less likely to see the lack of visible minority MPs as a serious problem (12 points).

These conclusions all rest on our simulations of how opinion might look if all Canadians were equally well informed. However, we can also draw on an actual experience of collective decision making to illustrate why aggregation does not necessarily compensate for shortfalls in information. In the case of the referendum on the Charlottetown Accord, lack of information hurt the "yes" side more than the "no" side (Johnston et al. 1996). Aggregation did not work because a critical presupposition of the aggregationist argument was not fulfilled. For aggregation to work, information must be unrelated to the direction of opinion.

This condition was clearly not met in the vote on the Charlottetown Accord. On the contrary, there was a strong relationship between information and vote choice: the more voters knew, the more likely they were to vote "yes." Controlling for education, support for the "yes" side outside Quebec was 20 points higher among the most informed than it was among the least informed. If the least informed had been as informed as the most informed, the "yes" side would have had a majority. Well-informed voters not only took different positions from poorly informed voters, they took different positions *because* they were well informed. Feelings toward the key negotiating partner – Canada in Quebec, and Quebec in the rest of Canada – help to explain the connection between information and vote choice. Outside Quebec, informed voters were more likely to feel positive about Quebec, and those positive feelings encouraged a "yes" vote. Similarly, inside Quebec, informed voters were more likely to feel positively about Canada, and those positive feelings also encouraged a "yes" vote.

Information narrowed the differences among social groups. Some of these effects were very substantial. In the case of regional differences, for example, a 30 point spread among low-information voters shrank to a 10 point spread among their high-information counterparts. And a 10 point gender gap among low-information voters all but disappeared among high-information voters, as the "yes" share among men came to resemble the "yes" share among women. In each case, the group differences diminished or disappeared because information increased the "yes" share. Seemingly, "knowing more actively changed voters' calculus by taking them out of the group and into a larger forum" (Johnston et al. 1996, 284).

The vote on the Charlottetown Accord drives home an important point: information is not necessarily directionally neutral. Rather than being random, the opinions of people who lack information may be systematically different from those of their well-informed counterparts. When this is true, aggregation will fail to compensate for shortfalls in information.

Getting It Wrong: Are Canadians Misinformed about Politics?

To this point, our focus has been on exploring the various implications of being uninformed about politics. When people are uninformed, they are simply unaware of the facts. But what if some Canadians are not so much *un*informed as *mis*informed? When people are misinformed, they have got the facts completely wrong. Kuklinski and his colleagues (2000, 793) spell out this important distinction: "To be *in*formed requires, first, that people have factual beliefs and, second, that the beliefs be accurate. If people do not hold factual beliefs at all, they are merely *un*informed ... But if they firmly hold beliefs that happen to be wrong, they are *mis*informed – not just in the dark, but wrongheaded." The difference between being uninformed and being misinformed has potentially far-reaching implications. When citizens base their policy positions on objectively false information, the result may well be "collective preferences that differ significantly from those that would exist if people were adequately informed" (Kuklinski et al. 2000, 792).

Indeed, being misinformed may have even more serious consequences than being uninformed. This is particularly true of policy-relevant information. As Delli Carpini and Keeter (1996, 11) argue: "Such facts as the percentage of the ... public living below the poverty line, how the line is determined, and how the percentage has changed over time provide a foundation for deliberation about larger issues. They prevent debates from becoming disconnected from the material conditions they attempt to address." If citizens hold objectively inaccurate beliefs about the relevant facts, policy debate will be not merely uninformed, but misinformed.

If the consequences of being misinformed are potentially so serious, two questions need to be explored. First, how widespread is misinformation in Canada? And second, what impact does misinformation have on policy preferences and electoral outcomes? The 1997 Canadian Election Study posed four questions that were deliberately designed to get at issue-specific misinformation. Canadians were asked about crime, pollution, poverty, and the situation of Aboriginal peoples:

Crime: "Do you think that crime in Canada has gone up, gone down or stayed about the same in the last few years?"
Pollution: "Do you think that pollution in Canada has got worse, got better or stayed about the same in the last few years?"
Poverty: "Do you think the gap between rich and poor in Canada has increased, decreased, or stayed about the same over the last few years?"
Aboriginal peoples: "In general, would you say that Canada's Aboriginal peoples are better off, worse off, or about the same as other Canadians?"

Crime was clearly on the decline in 1997: Canada's police-reported crime rate had dropped for the sixth consecutive year to produce the lowest crime rate since 1980 (Canadian Centre for Justice Statistics 1997). Rates of violent crime, property crime, and youths charged with Criminal Code offences all showed decreases for the fifth consecutive year (or more). Pollution was also diminishing. Urban air quality, for example, was better than it had been five years previously (Environment Canada 1999). On the other hand, the gap between the rich and the poor in Canada (as indicated by wealth inequality) had been increasing (Morissette, Zhang, and Drolet 2002), and Canada's Aboriginal peoples clearly remained worse off than the population at large. According to the 1996 census, the percentage of families at or below Statistics Canada's low income cut-offs was 40.9 percent for status Indians and 40.3 percent for status Indians living on reserve, compared with 16.5 percent for the total population of Canada (Indian and Northern Affairs Canada 2000). Meanwhile, the unemployment rate was 27.2 percent for status Indians and 28.7 percent for status Indians living on reserve, compared with 10.1 percent for the Canadian population as a whole. Finally, life expectancy was 68.2 years for status Indian men but 75.7 years for Canadian men in general. The comparable figures for female life expectancy were 75.9 years and 81.5 years. (Separate figures are not available for status Indians living on reserve.)

As Figure 4.3 shows, misperceptions about these conditions were widespread. Only one-third of those interviewed responded that Aboriginal peoples are worse off. Close to 60 percent incorrectly stated that Aboriginal peoples are better off or about the same, despite unequivocal evidence to the contrary. Levels of misinformation were even higher when it came to pollution and the crime rate. The vast majority of respondents were wrong on both counts. Fewer than one in ten knew that crime had actually decreased in Canada over the last few years and fewer than one in five knew that the same was true of pollution. Even if we adopt a more generous standard and count as misinformed only those who thought that crime (59 percent) or pollution (43 percent) had gone up, the conclusion is still crystal clear: many Canadians held beliefs that were quite at odds with the facts. On

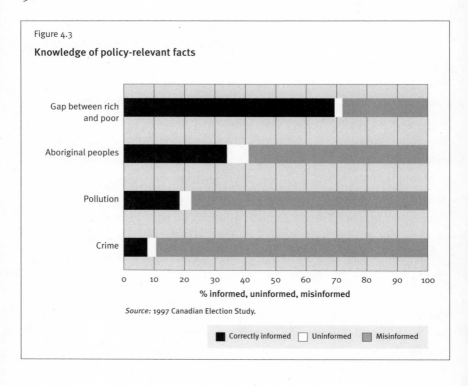

Figure 4.3

Knowledge of policy-relevant facts

% informed, uninformed, misinformed

Source: 1997 Canadian Election Study.

■ Correctly informed   ☐ Uninformed   ▨ Misinformed

only one question out of the four (the gap between the rich and the poor) did a majority get the facts straight, and even then, well over a quarter failed to realize that the gap had been increasing.

Given what we know about information (see Chapter 3), there is no reason to suppose that misinformation is evenly distributed throughout the population. The question, then, is who is most susceptible to misinformation? To some extent, the answer depends on the topic. For example, women were more misinformed than men about crime (92 percent versus 86 percent) and pollution (82 percent versus 73 percent), but not about poverty and the condition of Aboriginal peoples. Age made a difference only for pollution: younger Canadians were more likely to get it wrong. People with lower incomes were more likely to be misinformed, even allowing for differences in educational attainment. Ironically, this pattern even extends to the gap between the rich and the poor: fully a third of low-income Canadians appeared to be unaware that the gap had been increasing, compared with only a quarter of high-income Canadians. The single exception to this pattern concerns the situation of Aboriginal peoples: there was no significant difference in misinformation across income groups, once other relevant factors were taken into account. Education, on the other hand, had a particularly powerful effect on misinformation about the plight of Aboriginal peoples. Fully 70 percent of those who failed to complete high school got the facts wrong, compared with 40 percent of university graduates. Pollution was the only issue of the four where education failed to reduce the level of misinformation.

It is reasonable to speculate that media exposure would help people to be correctly informed. However, media consumption does little to diminish misinformation on these four questions. The single exception, once again, concerns the situation of Aboriginal peoples. The more attention people reported paying to the media, the more likely they were to get the facts right. This pattern held for television news, the press, and radio alike, but the effect was quite modest, even in the absence of controls. Far more striking is the absence of a similar effect for pollution, crime, or the gap between rich and poor. The mass media, it seems, do little to help correct the widespread misperceptions that exist.

While misinformation was widespread on these issues, it could be countered by political expertise. Political expertise seems to help people sort facts from fiction (Nadeau et al. 2002b). The more people knew about politics in general, the less likely they were to be misinformed about trends in pollution, the gap between the rich and the poor, or the condition of Aboriginal peoples (see Figure 4.4). Having a store of general knowledge about politics made the least difference for the item that elicited the most erroneous responses: the well informed were only a little less likely than the uninformed to know that crime had actually been going down. The knowledge effect was strongest for the situation of Canada's Aboriginal peoples: almost three-quarters of those who were ill informed about politics in general got the facts wrong, compared with fewer than half of the best informed. Political expertise also had a substantial effect on knowledge of the gap

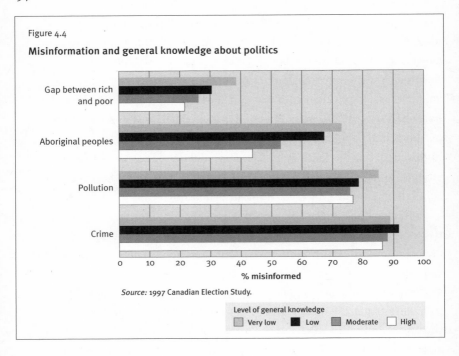

Figure 4.4

Misinformation and general knowledge about politics

Source: 1997 Canadian Election Study.

between the rich and the poor: almost two-fifths of the uninformed failed to realize that the gap had been growing, compared with less than a quarter of the well informed.

All of these effects remained statistically significant, even after social background characteristics and different types of political involvement, like interest in politics and media consumption, were taken into account. The implication is that something about having a general stock of political information per se makes people less prone to misinformation. Perhaps people who are well informed have simply been more likely to encounter the true facts. Certainly, having such a store of general knowledge about politics helps people to make sense of and to retain new information (Price and Zaller 1993; Nadeau et al. 2002a). The fact of the matter, however, is that even people who are generally well informed about politics can be prone to misinformation. Political expertise reduces the amount of policy-relevant misinformation, but it does not eliminate it.

These high levels of public misinformation are not peculiar to Canada. Studies in the United States have documented substantial levels of misinformation about a variety of public policy issues, including HIV transmission (Price and Hsu 1992), minority groups (Nadeau, Niemi, and Levine 1993; Nadeau and Niemi 1995), racial inequality and environmental protection (Keeter 1996), and welfare policy (Kuklinski et al. 2000). For example, only about a third of respondents in a US survey could provide a reasonable estimate of the proportion of the US population that is Hispanic, and more than half got it plain wrong, typically overestimating the figure (Nadeau, Niemi, and Levine 1993).

Given that there can be substantial levels of misinformation, the next question becomes: does misinformation matter? Evidence from the United States suggests that it does. Kuklinski and his colleagues (2000), for example, found that mistaken beliefs about welfare were not only widespread but skewed collective opinion in an antiwelfare direction. The erroneous beliefs were held confidently and resisted correction. People had to be "hit between the eyes" with the real facts for them to change their minds about welfare spending. To the extent that people base their policy preferences on what they perceive to be the "facts" of the situation, we can reasonably assume that their preferences might differ if they had more accurate information.

A number of items included in the 1997 Canadian Election Study enable us to examine whether misinformation leads to similar biases in Canadians' policy preferences (see Nadeau et al. 2002a). Respondents were asked whether spending on welfare should be cut and how much should be done to reduce the gap between rich and poor Canadians. They were also queried about their desired level of spending for Aboriginal peoples, the best way to deal with young offenders, and whether protecting the environment is more important than creating jobs. Notice that the foci of these policy issue questions corresponds to the policy foci of the questions used to gauge misinformation.

As Figure 4.5 shows, many people who are misinformed would take different stands if they had the facts straight. For example, almost half of those who realized that Aboriginal Canadians are worse off favoured more federal spending for Aboriginal peoples, compared with

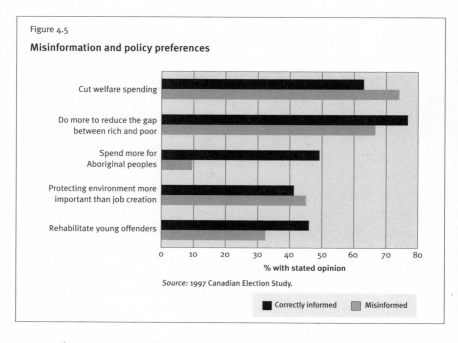

Figure 4.5

Misinformation and policy preferences

% with stated opinion

Source: 1997 Canadian Election Study.

Legend: ■ Correctly informed ▨ Misinformed

only one in ten of those who got the facts wrong. And over three-quarters of those who knew that the gap between rich and poor was increasing thought that more should be done to reduce the gap, compared with only two-thirds of those who were misinformed. Misinformation also affected views about welfare spending: the misinformed were more likely to favour cuts than those who knew the facts. Meanwhile, barely a third of those who were unaware that crime was going down favoured the rehabilitation of young offenders, compared with close to half of those who got it right. Misinformation made much less difference (4 points) to views about the trade-off between protecting the environment and creating jobs, but the difference remained statistically significant in the presence of an array of controls (Nadeau et al. 2002b). Misinformation can clearly skew collective policy preferences: how much depends on the issue at hand.

Misinformation does not produce random policy preferences. If so, its effects would be more benign because the misinformed preferences would cancel one another out. On the contrary, the biases are quite systematic. If people believe that Aboriginal peoples are better off than other Canadians, they are hardly likely to say that federal spending for Aboriginal peoples should be increased. Similarly, if people think that crime has been increasing in Canada, they are more likely to favour a get-tough approach. And if they think that poverty is diminishing, they are more likely to favour cuts in welfare spending. Clearly, then, we cannot count on the process of aggregation to filter out the preferences of those who are misinformed.

Far from correcting for misinformation, the use of information shortcuts may actually be a source of misinformation. It is not difficult to imagine how information shortcuts could lead a person astray. A random spate of crime in the neighbourhood, for example, could easily lead a person to infer quite wrongly that crime in general is going up. Similarly, voting retrospectively on the basis of the incumbent government's performance will not necessarily avoid the misinformation problem. Voters may not be accurately informed about what the government has been doing.

Indeed, voters' perceptions about past government performance can be just as prone to error as their perceptions of policy-relevant conditions. Evidence from the 1997 federal election provides a case in point. At the time of the election, the vast majority (81 percent) of Canadians wrongly believed that unemployment levels had *not* gone down during the tenure of the Liberal government, and nearly 40 percent actually thought that unemployment had increased. This misperception mattered: the probability of voting Liberal was 8 points higher among those who (rightly) perceived that unemployment had gone down than it was among those who (wrongly) thought that it had been on the rise. And this piece of misinformation cost the Liberals votes (Nadeau et al. 2000). A more detailed analysis indicates that the Liberal vote share would have been 3 points higher had it not been for the widespread misperception about unemployment. And that difference would have been enough to erase much of the Liberals' loss of seats in Parliament.

Election campaigns are opportunities for citizens to learn the political facts that will help them decide how to vote. But does the information circulating during an election campaign help to correct misperceptions, or does it actually increase the level of misinformation among the electorate? Ideally, election campaigns should reach the least attentive and least informed members of the population and help to correct their misperceptions. Our analysis of the 1997 federal election campaign indicated that the election campaign failed on both counts. The campaign did little to correct misperceptions about unemployment. Voters were no better informed about the Liberals' performance on the jobs front at the end of the campaign than they had been at the beginning.

This is not surprising. The Liberals chose not to campaign on their record of job creation. Unemployment had dropped 2 points during their term in office, but still remained close to 10 percent. Having hammered the theme of "jobs, jobs, jobs" in the 1993 election, the Liberals may have felt that it would be risky to play up the issue. Meanwhile, the opposition parties encouraged the perception that the number of unemployed had barely dropped during the Liberals' tenure. For example, Reform leader Preston Manning claimed that the prime minister had failed to keep his 1993 campaign promise to give priority to job creation, while his NDP counterpart, Alexa McDonough, was reported telling a labour convention "that the current unemployment numbers are almost identical to those posted when Mr. Chrétien took office in 1993" (Little 1997, A9). Voters therefore had little to learn from a campaign that failed to inform them of the facts. Indeed, attentiveness was of little help in getting it right about unemployment. Neither education nor general knowledge about politics nor media consumption made voters any more likely to correctly perceive that unemployment had gone down during the Liberal mandate (Nadeau et al. 2000).

Instead, voters apparently drew on their personal experiences (whether they were unemployed or worried about keeping their job), the local context (the unemployment rate in their province), or partisan cues (whether or not they identified with the Liberal Party) to inform their general judgments about unemployment (Nadeau et al. 2000). This was true of the attentive and the inattentive alike. Reliance on these contextual and attitudinal cues, however, often led to erroneous conclusions about the unemployment situation in the country.

Discussion

On some issues, aggregation does seem to compensate for shortfalls in information. Even if people were better informed, the majority position on these issues would be unlikely to change. But aggregation can only compensate for information shortfalls if information – or rather lack of information – is evenly distributed throughout the population and if information per se is unrelated to opinion. When one or both of these conditions fails to hold, collective expressions of public opinion will not accurately reflect the mix of wants and needs in Canadian society. As we have seen, opinion might well differ on some significant questions of public policy if Canadians were better informed about politics. Equally clearly, the uneven social distribution of information plays an important role in skewing public opinion on these issues. White, middle-aged, affluent men are more likely to see their needs and wants reflected in collective expressions of opinion, especially on questions of social policy.

The fact that aggregation works for some issues suggests that information shortcuts may well be helping some people to get to the "right" position. Even if they were better informed, their opinions on these issues would probably not change. On other issues, this is clearly not the case. Information shortcuts do not necessarily help poorly informed voters to translate their needs and wants into the appropriate political choices. This is because the people who need these shortcuts the most are often the least able to benefit from them. An information shortcut cannot compensate for shortfalls in information if people are so politically unaware that they lack the contextual information required to take the shortcut.

This brings us to another critical dimension of political ignorance. Many Canadians are misinformed about policy-relevant facts. Large numbers of Canadians get the facts wrong about the condition of

Canada's Aboriginal peoples and whether crime and pollution and the gap between rich and poor have increased or decreased in recent years. Levels of erroneous information are surprisingly high, and this misinformation matters because inaccurate beliefs affect people's policy preferences. Were it not for misinformation about policy-relevant facts, collective opinion in Canada would be more open to increased spending for Aboriginal peoples and the rehabilitation of young offenders, and there would be less support for cuts to welfare spending. At the same time, people might profess less willingness to trade off jobs for environmental protection.

Finally, it is surely worth emphasizing that not only do poorer Canadians stand at the economic margins of society, they also stand at the information margins; they are the most likely to be misinformed. This is true even regarding the gap between the rich and the poor. And again, the unequal social distribution of political information clearly matters. When poorer Canadians are misinformed about the gap between the rich and the poor in Canada, they are less likely to support action to alleviate the situation. This drives home an important point: information shortfalls can pose a real threat to the responsiveness of our political system.

Chapter 4

- Aggregation does not always compensate for shortfalls in information. Informed opinion tends to be systematically different from actual opinion. Informed opinion on social policy questions tends to be more liberal than actual opinion, and so does opinion on questions dealing with fiscal policy and the role of the state.

- White, middle-aged, affluent men are the most likely to see their needs and interests reflected in collective expressions of opinion.

- The use of information shortcuts does not necessarily compensate for shortfalls in information. The people who need the shortcuts the most are the least likely to be in a position to use them.

- Many Canadians are misinformed about basic policy-relevant facts like the gap between the rich and the poor and the condition of Canada's Aboriginal peoples.

- Misinformation skews policy preferences. If Canadians were not misinformed, public opinion would be more favourable to spending for Aboriginal peoples and to rehabilitating young offenders, and there would be less willingness to cut welfare spending or to trade off jobs for environmental protection.

- Misinformation is not confined to policy-relevant facts, but extends to more general knowledge relating to government performance.

5

HOW MUCH DO CANADIANS PARTICIPATE IN POLITICS?

No democratic audit would be complete without an evaluation of political participation. The focus here is on two key themes. The first concerns who participates in the democratic process and, more important, who does not. This information is critical to assessing Canada's democratic performance against the benchmarks of inclusiveness and responsiveness; knowing who is a part of Canada's political life and who is left out tells us whose voices are most likely to be heard and whose may get ignored. The second theme concerns *how* Canadians participate; political participation is not all of a piece. Some forms of political participation, such as turning out to vote in elections at different levels of government, demand little of citizens. Others, such as joining a political party or an interest group, demand much more. At the same time, voting and joining political parties and interest groups are all very conventional types of participation. Less conventional types of political activity, such as participating in an illegal strike or joining in a political protest, also deserve attention.

How Many Canadians Are Exercising Their Right to Vote in Federal Elections?

The right to vote in free and open elections is one of the defining characteristics of a representative democracy. Citizens in established democracies are apt to take that right for granted; they forget that people around the globe have laid down their lives to win this right. Indeed, in many countries the struggle to establish free and fair voting for citizens continues to this day. Free and open elections are essential prerequisites to democratic life because they provide citizens with an opportunity both to hold their elected representatives accountable for their actions and to authorize future policy directions.

Voting in elections is not very demanding of citizens; it takes little time and energy, and elections are not that frequent. For many Canadians it is their only form of political participation. But if citizens cannot be bothered to exercise this most basic of democratic rights, there is surely cause for concern. "Not to vote," as Putnam (2000, 35) bluntly puts it, "is to withdraw from the political community." Putnam likens levels of voter turnout to the canary that coal miners used to take down into the pit. Just as the canary could warn the miners of impending danger, so declining turnout can alert us to deeper structural changes that could ultimately threaten the country's democratic health.

Between 1945 and 1988, turnout in Canadian federal elections averaged 75.4 percent, varying between a high of 79.4 percent in 1958 and a low of 67.9 percent in 1953 (see Figure 5.1). The Canadian average of 75.4 percent turns out to be more than 10 points lower than the median average turnout of 86.2 percent for the entire group of Anglo-American, Nordic, and West European democracies over the same period (excluding Australia and Belgium, which both have compulsory voting) (see Pintor and Gratschew 2002). In that group of countries, average turnout ranged from a low of 56.4 percent in US presidential elections to a high of 93.6 percent in Austrian parliamentary elections. Canadian levels of voter turnout during this period were comparable to those of publics in Finland (77.9 percent), France (76.9

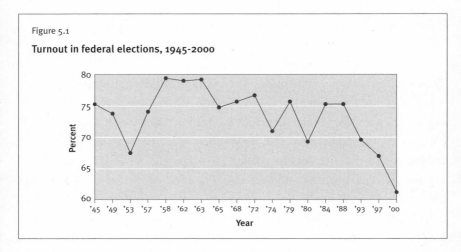

Figure 5.1

Turnout in federal elections, 1945-2000

percent), the UK (76.5 percent), and Ireland (74.1 percent). There seem to be two explanations for why Canada's turnout is below the average (Blais and Dobrzynska 1998; Black 1991). The first has to do with Canada's single-member plurality electoral system (see Courtney 2004). In this type of system, turnout tends to be about 3 points lower on average than in systems based on proportional representation. The second part of the explanation concerns demography: turnout tends to be lower in large, thinly populated countries.

Turnout in Canadian federal elections has fallen dramatically since 1988, by some 14 points. In the 2000 federal election, only 61 percent of registered voters bothered to cast their ballot (though actual turnout was about 64 percent once duplicate names were removed from the list). Not surprisingly, that historical low prompted considerable speculation about why voter turnout levels were dropping so sharply, and pundits have pointed the finger at everything from problems with the new permanent voters list to a rising tide of political cynicism to what Stephen Clarkson (2001) has dubbed the Liberal "threepeat." None of these explanations, however, survives critical scrutiny.

For any citizen to be able to vote, his or her name has to be correctly entered on the voters list (Black 2000; Courtney 2004). Until the 2000 election, the standard practice was that Elections Canada drew up a new voters list for each election. Enumerators visited every household in the country to obtain the names of eligible voters. The 2000 election was the first election in which a permanent voters list replaced door-to-door enumeration. Elections Canada and various federal and provincial government agencies share information electronically to make sure that the list is up to date. For example, federal income tax returns now include a box that citizens can check to indicate that they authorize the Canada Customs and Revenue Agency to provide their name, address, and date of birth to Elections Canada for the National Register of Electors. When young Canadians turn eighteen years old, they automatically receive a card from Elections Canada asking them to inform Elections Canada if they do not agree to having their name added to the list. Then, once an election is called, Elections Canada sends out voter information cards to everyone whose name appears on the list.

Despite all of these efforts, many eligible voters discovered that they were not on the list in 2000; others failed to receive their card. To compound the problem, many of these people were unaware that they could register throughout the election campaign and indeed on the day of the election itself. According to the 2000 Canadian Election Study, one respondent in six had not received a voter information card. Of these respondents, close to two in five reported difficulties in getting their name on the voters list. Undeniably there were some problems with the implementation of the permanent voters list, but these problems cannot explain the decline in turnout for a simple reason: voter turnout was clearly declining in the two previous elections as well, that is, *before* the switch to the permanent voters list (see Centre for Research and Information on Canada 2001).

What about the Liberal "threepeat" explanation? This argument suggests that turnout declined because the outcome of the election was more or less a foregone conclusion. The assumption here is that people are less likely to vote if they think that their vote will not make any difference to the outcome. If a third straight Liberal victory was assured, the argument goes, why should people bother to go to the polls? The evidence shows that while a relationship exists between the closeness of an election and voter turnout, the link is not very strong (Blais and Dobrzynska 1998). Other things being equal, turnout will typically be about 3 points higher when an election is extremely close than when the margin of victory is 15 points, as it was in 2000. But then again, other things are not always equal. The 1958 federal election resulted in a Conservative landslide *and* a record high turnout. Conversely, the 1957 federal election produced a Conservative minority but only an average turnout.

The 2000 Canadian Election Study asked Canadians to estimate each party's chance of winning in their constituency. Few people thought that one party was certain to win, and the perceived closeness of the race had only a marginal effect on whether they voted (Blais et al. 2002). The Liberal "threepeat" argument essentially says that many people stayed home because the election was simply not very interesting. Whether this is a fair characterization of the 2000 election is certainly open to debate (see Centre for Research and Information on Canada 2001), but the larger point remains: turnout declined in the 1993 and 1997 elections as well. By no stretch of the imagination could the 1993 federal election, with the breakthrough of two new political parties – the Reform Party and the Bloc Québécois – and the near collapse of two established parties – the Progressive Conservatives and the NDP – be described as boring.

Some election postmortems in 2000 linked declining voter turnout since 1988 to the rise in political disaffection, itself symptomatic of a deeper democratic malaise. The extent of Canadians' disaffection with politics should not be underestimated (Blais and Gidengil 1991; Howe and Northrup 2000). At the time of the 2000 election, for example, almost two-thirds of Canadians agreed that "The government does not care much what people like me think." The problem with this diagnosis of declining turnout revolves around timing. Political disaffection increased in the 1970s and 1980s (see Figure 5.2), but turnout started to decline only in the 1990s. If anything, levels of political discontent seem to have declined in the late 1990s after peaking earlier in the decade. Other indicators of political disaffection like trust in govern-

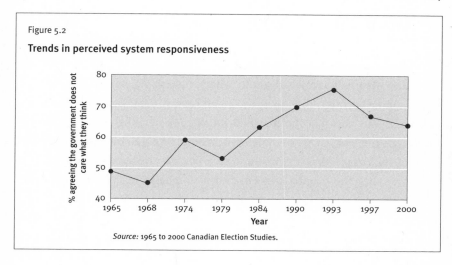

Figure 5.2

Trends in perceived system responsiveness

Source: 1965 to 2000 Canadian Election Studies.

ment, confidence in the House of Commons, and confidence in political parties show a similar pattern. In any case, closer analysis shows that political disaffection does not have much independent impact on turnout to vote (Blais et al. 2002). While some Canadians are simply turned off by politics, others may be motivated to vote if only to "throw the rascals out."

The falling turnout in recent federal elections is not a peculiarly Canadian phenomenon, and this has important implications. Between 1990 and 2000, turnout declined in thirteen of the fifteen Anglo-American, Nordic, and West European democracies without compulsory voting (the only countries to buck the trend were Sweden and Denmark). The average decline was almost 9 percentage points. In nine countries, turnout in the most recent national election was the lowest recorded in the entire postwar period. The median average turnout in elections held between 1990 and 2000 for the fifteen countries was 77.0 percent, down 9.2 percentage points from the median for the 1945 to 1989 period. Deeper structural factors may thus be contributing to the decline in turnout in Canadian federal elections. One way to try to understand these factors is to consider the nonvoters (see Blais et al. 2002).

Who Are the Nonvoters?

As we have seen, women tend to be less interested in politics than men and also less informed about what is going on politically. Even so, women turn out to vote at the same rate as men. Indeed, once differences in political interest and knowledge of politics are taken into account, women are actually a little more likely than men to vote. Part of the reason is that women tend to have a stronger sense of duty to vote than men, and a sense of moral obligation is a powerful motivating factor when it comes to voting (see Blais 2000).

In many Western democracies, religion and union membership have proved to be strong mobilizing forces. The impact of religion on turnout seems to be weakening in Canada. Once other social background characteristics are taken into account, people's likelihood of voting in the 2000 election was little affected by whether they described themselves as religious or secular. Similarly, people who belonged to union households were no more likely to vote than those who came from nonunion households. This may well reflect the weakness of class-based voting in Canada (Gidengil 2002).

But people's material circumstances are not irrelevant. On the contrary, household income is an important determinant of turnout. According to the 2000 Canadian Election Study, turnout was 16 points lower among people with household incomes in the bottom 20 percent than it was among those in the top 20 percent. Even when other possible differences between the rich and the poor are taken into account, a significant gap in turnout remains. Studies of voter turnout in a number of other countries reveal a similar gap (see Blais 2000; Norris 2002).

Poverty depresses turnout for several reasons. The costs associated with voting are modest, but they may be enough of an obstacle to deter some people from voting if they are trying to make a social assistance cheque stretch to the end of the month. And people living at the edge of poverty may simply have less time and energy for politics. They may also feel that they do not have much of a stake in a political system that fails to address their needs and concerns. Finally, poorer Canadians may be more affected than others by the problems with the permanent voters list (Black 2000). One reason is that they are more likely to be living in rented accommodation. Tenants are less likely than home-owners to be correctly registered in the constituency where they live because they change addresses more frequently. Moreover, the new system puts the onus on voters to get their name added to the list, which requires both time and information.

Whether people live in rural areas or urban areas has little impact on turnout. The same is true of place of birth. Whether people were born in Canada or came to Canada as immigrants makes little differ-ence to their odds of voting. What does matter is when they came: peo-ple who have been in the country for ten years or less are much less likely to vote. This is hardly surprising. There is inevitably an adjust-ment process as newcomers seek to establish themselves in unfamil-iar surroundings. Once established, though, new Canadians are as likely to vote as those who are Canadian born. The same cannot be said of members of visible minorities. Canadian born or not, they are less likely to vote than other Canadians. The main reason has to do with age: the proportion of people in their twenties is especially high in this segment of the population.

Indeed, the single most important determinant of voting is age. According to the 2000 Canadian Election Study, turnout was as much as 30 points lower among Canadians born since 1970 than among those born before 1945. Lower turnout among young people is not a new finding. Detailed analyses of nonvoting in federal elections going back to 1968 indicate that the likelihood of voting increases by 7 or 8 points between the ages of twenty and thirty, by 4 to 6 points between the ages of thirty and forty, and by 2 or 3 points between the ages of forty and fifty (Blais et al. 2004). Turnout tends to remain stable when people are in their fifties and sixties, but as citizens enter their seven-ties, decreased mobility and deteriorating health begin to take their toll and voter turnout drops off. All in all, these life-cycle effects increase turnout by about 15 points between age twenty and age fifty.

It is easy to understand why the largest jump in turnout occurs as people move from their twenties into their thirties (see Baum 2002). At this stage of their lives, people are most likely to marry or settle down with a partner, to become parents, to settle into a job, and to buy a home. As taxes, mortgage rates, and access to health care take on a new significance, people may well have a growing sense that politics matters. Also, putting down roots in the community exposes young adults to social pressures that encourage a feeling that they *ought* to vote.

Important as these life-cycle effects are, they do not explain away the gap in turnout. The generation of Canadians born since 1970 is less likely to vote than their parents or grandparents were when they were the same age. Turnout among the post-1970 generation is 10 points lower than it was among those born in the 1960s when they were in their twenties and 20 points lower than it was among baby boomers at the same age (Blais et al. 2004). Indeed, much of the decline in voter turnout among Canadians since 1988 is attributable to generational replacement.

Figure 5.3 tracks trends in voting for the pre-baby boomers (born before 1945), the baby boomers (born between 1945 and 1959), generation X (born in the 1960s), and the post-generation X (born since 1970). Turnout among the oldest generation in 1988 is used as the benchmark. In 1988, few members of the youngest generation were old enough to vote, so we start tracking them in 1993. The results are truly striking: the decline in turnout is almost wholly confined to the youngest generation. The three older generations show no consistent trends in turnout. If the relative weight of the generations had remained the same in 2000 as it was in 1988, turnout in the 2000 federal election would have been 10 points higher. So to understand why turnout is going down, we have to focus on those born since 1970.

The declining turnout in this generation poses a puzzle. Education is a strong correlate of turnout: the more schooling people have, the more likely they are to vote. Education equips people with the cognitive skills needed to navigate the complexities of politics, and it fosters norms of civic engagement, including a sense of duty to vote.

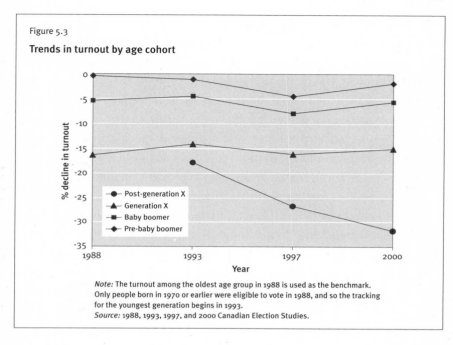

Figure 5.3

Trends in turnout by age cohort

Note: The turnout among the oldest age group in 1988 is used as the benchmark. Only people born in 1970 or earlier were eligible to vote in 1988, and so the tracking for the youngest generation begins in 1993.
Source: 1988, 1993, 1997, and 2000 Canadian Election Studies.

Today's young Canadians enjoy unprecedented access to postsecondary education, so why are they voting less than their parents or their grandparents did when they were in their twenties?

Education does indeed make a massive difference to whether young Canadians vote. The 2000 Canadian Election Study data show that turnout in the youngest generation was almost 50 points higher among university graduates than among those who left school without a high school diploma. The decline in turnout is in fact confined to those with less than a university education; turnout has held steady among young graduates. Since the 1993 federal election, turnout has dropped over 30 points among those with less than a high school education and 15 points or more among those who have completed high school or some postsecondary education. So why are younger, less educated Canadians so much less likely to vote? Are they turned off or simply tuned out?

The answer seems to be: tuned out. Canadians born since 1970 are no more disaffected with politics than older Canadians (O'Neill 2001).

Indeed, if anything, they are a little *less* so. But young Canadians are much less interested in politics and know much less about what is going on politically than Canadians who are thirty and over. And political interest and political knowledge are two of the strongest correlates of turnout to vote; both enhance people's motivation to vote. Moreover, knowledge makes the act of voting easier: knowing about the issues, where the parties stand, and who the leaders are makes it easier to decide which party to vote for. Lack of interest and lack of knowledge are clearly an important part of the explanation for why so many young Canadians are staying away from the polling stations. Had younger Canadians been as interested in politics and as informed as older Canadians, their turnout in the 2000 federal election would have been 14 points higher.

Interest is a two-way street: the less effort political parties and their candidates make to mobilize voters, the less likely they are to vote. If people were contacted by *any* of the parties during the 2000 election campaign, their odds of voting increased significantly. And young Canadians were the least likely to have been contacted: fewer than one in three reported any contact by a party or a candidate, compared with half the baby boomers and pre-baby boomers. One reason may be that young people are harder to reach because they tend to be more mobile.

The introduction of the permanent voters list in the 2000 federal election also had a disproportionate impact on young citizens. Fully one in three of those born since 1970 told us that they did not receive a voter information card, compared with fewer than one in five of those born in the 1960s and only one in ten of those born earlier. Moreover, in the youngest age group fully half of those who did not receive a card said it was difficult to get their name added to the list.

Another part of the explanation for the high rate of nonvoting among young Canadians is a diminished sense of duty to vote. Fewer than one-fifth of those born since 1970 expressed a strong sense of duty to vote, compared with one-third of those born before 1945, and almost two-fifths said that they would not feel guilty at all if they did not vote, compared with only 15 percent of older Canadians. Why these young Canadians feel less of a moral obligation to vote is unclear, but it may have something to do with the fact that they came of age during a period of declining deference (Nevitte 1996).

Young citizens are not the only ones who are voting in ever decreasing numbers. There is evidence of a very significant decline in turnout to vote on the part of many Aboriginal peoples. Reliable data addressing the issue of Aboriginal turnout are remarkably scarce, but a study of voter turnout among on-reserve status Indians in the Maritime provinces by David Bedford and Sidney Pobihushchy (1995) provides some useful insights. They track trends in turnout in federal and provincial elections in polls wholly included within reserves, beginning with the 1962 election. Except for a brief interlude in the late 1880s, this was the first federal election in which status Indians were allowed to vote without having to give up their status (see Courtney 2004).

Between 1962 and 1988, federal voter turnout on Nova Scotia reserves declined from 89.3 percent to 54.0 percent. The decline was even steeper on New Brunswick reserves: turnout in federal elections plummeted from 70 percent in 1962 to a mere 17.8 percent in 1988. The trend was similar in provincial elections in the two provinces. Turnout in provincial elections dropped from 67.2 percent in 1967 to 45.2 percent in 1993 in Nova Scotia and from 64.4 percent in 1967 to 27.6 percent in 1991 in New Brunswick.

A study of First Nations voting on sixty-four Manitoba reserves tells a similar story (Kinnear 2003). Turnout in federal elections dropped from 65.4 percent in 1962 to 32.6 percent in 1997, though it did rise to 45.7 percent in 2000. Meanwhile, turnout in provincial elections has fallen from 53.5 percent in 1969 to 26.7 percent in 2003. First Nations turnout in provincial elections has also declined steeply in Saskatchewan and Alberta (Bedford 2003).

There is a good deal of variation, however, from province to province and community to community. Bedford and Pobihushchy (1995) reveal that turnout on reserves in the third Maritime province – Prince Edward Island – has been consistently higher in federal and provincial elections alike, though this may have something to do with the small size of the province's on-reserve population. Aboriginal turnout in Quebec provincial elections, by contrast, has been consistently low (Bedford 2003).

A detailed analysis of Aboriginal turnout in the 2000 federal election, using a methodology similar to Bedford and Pobihushchy's, identified three broad groupings (Guérin 2003). At 66.9 percent, turnout rates at polling stations on First Nations reserves were highest in Prince Edward Island. Saskatchewan (55.0 percent), Nunavut (54.3 percent), Alberta (53.9 percent), and British Columbia (51.3 percent) also qualified for the high-turnout group. The medium-turnout group consisted of the Northwest territories (45.9 percent), Ontario (44.5 percent), Newfoundland (43.7 percent), New Brunswick (40.8 percent), and Nova Scotia (40.7 percent). Manitoba (36.6 percent) and Quebec (35.3 percent) made up the low-turnout group.

Guérin (2003) suggests two possible explanations for the variation in Aboriginal turnout. On the one hand, it could reflect cultural differences and differences in social conditions. Aboriginal communities vary in the strength and nature of their indigenous political traditions and sense of nationhood; the perceived legitimacy of electoral participation will vary accordingly (Ladner 2003). On the other hand, this variation could be the result of differences in the electoral context. For example, the presence of Aboriginal candidates seems to lead to higher turnout rates in northern communities. A focus on issues of concern to Aboriginal people can also boost turnout. Ladner (2003) cites the example of the Plains Cree, who encouraged voting in the 2000 federal election as a deliberate strategy to assert their nationhood and defend their treaty rights in the face of a perceived threat from the Alliance party. This may help to explain why turnout rose on Manitoba reserves in that election.

Overall, the on-reserve turnout rate (47.8 percent) in the 2000 federal election was almost 16 points lower than the rate for the general population. The figure was undoubtedly much lower for Aboriginal people living in Canada's cities. Guérin (2003) cites a 2001 Ipsos-Reid survey indicating that the turnout rate for urban Aboriginals could have been as much as three times lower than for those living on reserves. And the turnout figures for the latter are probably over-stated. As Bedford and Pobihushchy (1995) note, significant numbers of reserve residents simply refuse to be enumerated. Moreover, some First Nations (such as Akwesasne) refuse to have polling stations on their reserves (Ladner 2003).

This underscores a fundamental point: low Aboriginal turnout is not simply a matter of "tuning out." True, a higher proportion of the Aboriginal population falls into the eighteen to twenty-four age group, but the "youth factor" cannot explain the gap in voter turnout between Aboriginal peoples and the general population (Guérin 2003). Lower turnout cannot be explained, either, by the fact that it typically takes several decades for newly enfranchised groups to vote at the same rate as other voters. Like Native Americans in the United States, Canada's Aboriginal peoples appear to be an exception to this rule: turnout was initially high, but then a steady decline set in (Kinnear 2003). We have to look elsewhere for explanations.

Bedford and Pobihushchy argue that the decline in turnout reflects "a rejection of the Canadian electoral process as an alien one, a politi-cal process of a state which is not their own" (1995, 269). Indeed, the very concept of electoral democracy is an alien one with no natural roots in Aboriginal cultures. Bedford and Pobihushchy make the point bluntly: "Aboriginal traditional ways had no politics as we currently understand it. There were no elections" (p. 268). Other commentators have pointed to distrust of the federal government (Cairns 2003; Hunter 2003). Hunter links this distrust to the fact that enfranchise-ment was long used as a means of assimilating First Nations people by requiring them to give up their status. She suggests, "Many First Nations people fear that the recent calls to participate in Canadian political processes are a modern manifestation of the assimilationist agenda" (p. 30). More fundamentally, electoral participation may be seen as incompatible with aspirations to deal with the Canadian gov-ernment on a nation-to-nation basis (Cairns 2003; Hunter 2003; Lad-ner 2003). Not coincidentally, voter turnout has fallen as Aboriginal consciousness has risen.

As these authors emphasize, a good deal more research is required before we can generalize with any confidence about patterns of turnout in the diverse contexts in which Aboriginal peoples live in Canada. This research might usefully extend to voting in band elections. Unlike federal and provincial elections, band elections in New Brunswick and Nova Scotia have been characterized by consistently high turnout, typically around 90 percent (Bedford and Pobihushchy 1995). Most status Indians belong to a band, and as band members they get to elect the band chief and councillors. In New Brunswick and Nova Scotia, at least, these elections are hotly contested. Bedford and Pobihushchy attribute this to the real power that the band chief and councillors typically wield on reserves in these two provinces: they administer all federal monies and determine who will receive band jobs.

It remains to be determined whether turnout in band elections is as high in other contexts. But these findings underline an important point: turnout is related to the perceived stakes. This reinforces Hunter's (2003, 32) observation that we need "to shift the focus from negative consideration of why Aboriginal people do not vote to the development of positive reasons for Aboriginal people to vote."

How Many Canadians Are Voting in Provincial and Territorial Elections?

So far, we have focused largely on voting in federal elections and on the important role that generational replacement has played in the sharp decline in turnout since 1988. Can we detect parallel trends in voting in provincial elections? The first thing to note is that turnout is typically higher in provincial elections than in federal elections, except in Ontario, Alberta, and Manitoba (see Figure 5.4). Similarly, in both the Yukon and the Northwest Territories (the creation of Nunavut is too recent to permit us to compare trends), turnout is higher in territorial elections than it is in federal elections. The difference in average turnout at the two levels is largest in Newfoundland and Labrador, Prince Edward Island, and the territories.

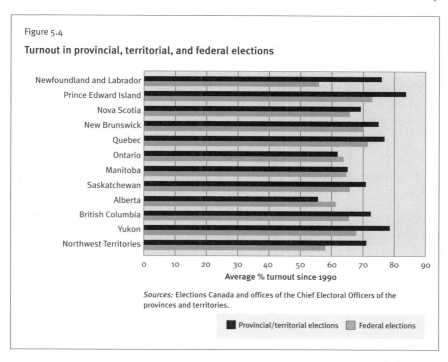

Figure 5.4

Turnout in provincial, territorial, and federal elections

Average % turnout since 1990

Sources: Elections Canada and offices of the Chief Electoral Officers of the provinces and territories.

Provincial/territorial elections ■ Federal elections ■

As Donley Studlar (2001) has pointed out, Canada is something of an anomaly in having higher turnout in subnational elections than in national elections.. To understand what he called "Canadian exceptionalism," Studlar studied provincial and federal turnout by province from 1945 to 1998. Social and cultural differences proved to be much more important than political factors in explaining variations across provinces in federal and provincial turnout.

There is a fairly widespread perception that multimember districts and greater proportionality in the translation of votes into seats encourage turnout. The assumption is that voters are less likely to think that their votes will be "wasted" when seats won correspond more closely to votes cast. Today, all federal and provincial elections are based on the single-member, first-past-the-post system, but this was not always the case. In the first half of the period examined by Studlar, there were multimember plurality electoral districts in almost every province, and Nova Scotia and Prince Edward Island each had a federal multimember district (see Courtney 2004 for details). Moreover, Alberta, British Columbia, and Manitoba had all tried preferential voting in provincial elections at one time or another. These electoral system differences, however, have had little discernible impact on turnout. The same is true of the (dis)proportionality of the results (in terms of the ratio of seats to votes).

Party-system features also make surprisingly little difference. One-party dominance does not have the expected effect of depressing turnout, though the difference between provincial election turnout and turnout in the closest federal election tends to be smaller when one party receives 55 percent or more of the vote in the provincial election. Meanwhile, the margin of victory seems to be a factor only in provincial elections. The higher the margin of victory enjoyed by the winning party, the lower turnout tends to be. A multiparty system does not significantly enhance turnout. In fact, multipartyism actually seems to decrease federal turnout. As Studlar (2001) notes, this is counterintuitive since the existence of more choices might be expected to encourage people to vote. The fact that political factors either fail to make a difference or have inconsistent effects suggests that institutional changes may have only a limited potential to fix the problem of low turnout.

Turnout is even lower in two other federal systems, Switzerland and the United States. This has been attributed to "election weariness." When elections are held too frequently, citizens are more apt to stay home. Studlar found some evidence of this. Turnout tends to be lower for provincial elections that are held close to the last federal election and for federal elections that are held close to the last provincial election. Turnout also tends to be lower, however, when there is a long lapse between federal elections.

Finally, population density affects turnout in federal elections. The more densely populated the province, the higher the turnout to vote in federal elections. This runs counter to the assumption that residence in rural communities encourages turnout. Studlar also found that the gap between provincial election turnout and turnout in the closest federal election was smaller in densely populated provinces. However, region was the most consistent predictor of turnout differences in federal and provincial elections. The turnout gap is significantly lower in Ontario and the West. This raises the question of what it is about these two regions that explains the similarity in turnout rates at the provincial and federal levels. Perhaps it has to do with regional political cultures, but precisely how do they account for the observed patterns? As Studlar concludes, a satisfactory account remains to be supplied.

The federal-provincial turnout gap is not the only puzzle. Since 1988, turnout in federal elections has dropped in every single province, the Yukon, and the Northwest Territories. In the Northwest Territories, Ontario, Saskatchewan, British Columbia, and the Yukon, the drop has been 15 points or more (turnout also fell by almost 15 points in Alberta, but from an atypically high level in 1988). At just over 8 points, the drop has been smallest in New Brunswick. Typically, much of the decline in turnout occurred between the 1988 and 1993 elections. The only exception was Quebec, where the advent of the Bloc Québécois induced many erstwhile abstainers in the province to vote. The effect was only temporary, however. By 2000 turnout was down 11 points in Quebec as well.

The decline in turnout has been less consistent in provincial elections, while turnout in territorial elections has remained fairly stable for the past two decades. Prince Edward Island and Alberta have also bucked the trend toward declining turnout. Prince Edward Island actually enjoyed a higher turnout in the 2000 provincial election (84.9 percent) than in the 1989 election (80.8 percent). Turnout in the 2001 Alberta provincial election, on the other hand, was very low (52.8 percent), but it was not nearly as low as it had been in the 1986 election when fewer than half (47.2 percent) of Albertans turned out to vote. Turnout in the 1999 Ontario election (58.3 percent) was close to the postwar low of 58.0 percent in the 1981 election, but it represented a drop of only 4 points since the 1987 election. And while turnout in British Columbia has dropped since the 1986 election, it remains higher than in most of the elections held between 1945 and 1979. At 11 points, the decline in turnout in Newfoundland and Labrador since the

1989 provincial election has been much steeper, but the 1999 turnout (69.6 percent) was still higher than the turnout in the four elections held between 1956 and 1966, and not much lower than the 1982 turnout (69.9 percent).

In Saskatchewan, though, turnout in provincial elections has dropped almost 17 points since the 1986 election. And in the remaining four provinces turnout in the most recent provincial election hit historical lows. At 53.9 percent, turnout in the 2003 Manitoba provincial election was the lowest recorded in half a century and represented a drop of over 14 points from the 1999 election. Turnout in the 2003 Quebec election was much higher at 70.5 percent, but this was down eight points from 1998 and represented the lowest turnout since the 1927 election. Meanwhile, turnout has been declining steadily in both New Brunswick and Nova Scotia. Turnout in the 2003 New Brunswick election (69.0 percent) was the lowest since record-keeping began in 1967, and was down 11 points from the 1991 election. Turnout in the 2003 Nova Scotia election (63.8 percent) was also the lowest since the province began to keep records in 1960, and was down 12 points since the 1988 election.

A case could be made that the four recent elections in Quebec, Manitoba, New Brunswick, and Nova Scotia all took place under unpropitious circumstances. The 2003 Quebec election coincided with the war in Iraq, while the other three elections all took place in the summer, when turnout is typically lower. It remains to be seen whether they herald a trend that will affect turnout in other provinces, too. And the puzzle remains why the decline in turnout has taken longer to show up – and has shown up less consistently – in provincial elections than in federal elections.

How Many Canadians Are Voting in Municipal Elections?

Lack of data is even more of a problem when it comes to fathoming turnout in municipal elections. Until recently, only Quebec centralized data on municipal elections. Ontario and Alberta now do so as well, but it is still extremely difficult to track trends in turnout or to compare turnout in different parts of the country or in different types of community. It is also difficult to make international comparisons of turnout in local elections. If the average turnout of around 50 percent in contested mayoral elections in Quebec, Ontario, and Alberta in the late 1990s was typical of municipal elections across the country, Canada ranked twelfth out of fifteen established Western democracies (Milner 2002).

There is only one published study of voting trends in municipal elections in Canada (Kushner, Siegel, and Stanwick 1997). Joseph Kushner and his colleagues obtained information on turnout by sending a questionnaire to municipal clerks in a representative sample of Ontario municipalities. Their results confirmed the conventional wisdom: turnout is typically lower in municipal elections than in either federal or provincial elections. As they note, comparisons of turnout in municipal and national elections in the United States and Europe indicate that higher turnout in national elections is the rule (Morland 1984). Where Canada differs is in the greater magnitude of the turnout gap. These findings call into question the notion that municipal politics is more salient to citizens than national politics because it deals with matters close to home like public security, recreation, garbage collection, roads, and sewers.

Kushner and colleagues report a significant association between the size of a municipality and the turnout to vote. Average voter turnout in 1994 in municipalities with a population of less than 10,000 was 54.0 percent, compared with 43.6 percent in municipalities with a population between 10,000 and 100,000, and a mere 37.0 percent in municipalities with a population of over 100,000. This fits well, they point out, with Verba and Nie's argument (1972, 231) that "in the small town ... citizens can know the ropes of politics, know whom to contact, know each other so that they can form political groups. In the larger units, politics is more complicated, impersonal, and distant ... Local participation becomes less and less meaningful." Indeed, Eric Oliver (2000) found that residents of larger US cities were less interested in local politics and less likely to have friends or neighbours who encouraged them to participate in local affairs. As a result, they were less likely to vote in local elections, contact local elected officials, or attend meetings of voluntary organizations and community boards.

Kushner and his colleagues (Kushner, Siegel, and Stanwick 1997) collected data on three elections – 1982, 1988, and 1994 – and found that turnout declined by about 3 percentage points across these elections. The drop in voter turnout was very similar in small, medium, and large municipalities. In order to get a sense of whether this was indicative of a more general trend, we requested figures on voter turnout for all municipal elections since 1945 from a number of cities. Seven cities were able to provide the requested information for some or all of the postwar period: Vancouver, Edmonton, Winnipeg (from 1971 onward), Hamilton (from 1962 onward), Toronto (from 1945 onward), Ottawa (from 1985 onward), and Montreal (from 1970 onward).

For these seven cities, at least, there is no evidence of a decline in voter turnout in recent years (see Figure 5.5). In Vancouver, turnout in the 1993, 1996, and 1999 elections was below the city's postwar average of 40.2 percent, but turnout was just as low in the four elections held between 1954 and 1960 and in the four elections held between 1972 and 1978. Meanwhile, in Edmonton, turnout dropped substantially in the two most recent elections, but it still remained just above the city's postwar average of 32.0 percent. Turnout in Hamilton in the 2000 election was just above the city's average for the 1962-2000 period (41.4 percent), while Winnipeg's turnout in the three most recent elections easily surpassed the average for the 1971-1998 period as a whole (46.1 percent). After dipping in the 1997 election, voter turnout in Ottawa's most recent election was well above the average of 37.8 percent for the 1985-2000 period, while Montreal's voter turnout rose steadily during the 1990s, before falling off very slightly in the first postmerger election in 2001. Finally, voter turnout in Toronto was close to the postwar average of 37.6 percent in three of the four elections held since 1990. The exception was the 1997 election: 52.8 percent of registered voters turned out to vote in the first postmerger election.

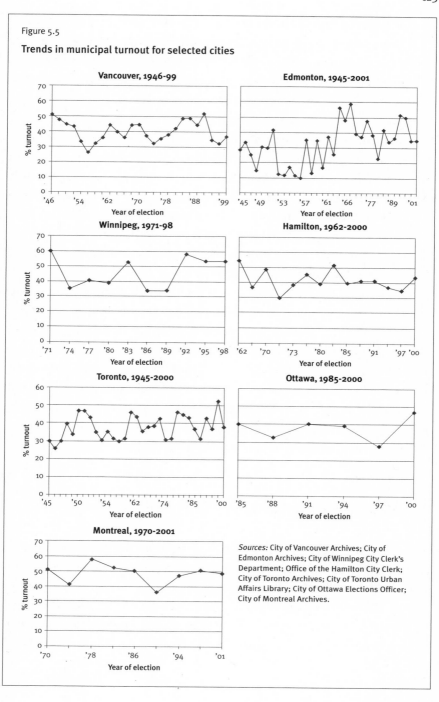

Figure 5.5

Trends in municipal turnout for selected cities

Vancouver, 1946-99

Edmonton, 1945-2001

Winnipeg, 1971-98

Hamilton, 1962-2000

Toronto, 1945-2000

Ottawa, 1985-2000

Montreal, 1970-2001

Sources: City of Vancouver Archives; City of Edmonton Archives; City of Winnipeg City Clerk's Department; Office of the Hamilton City Clerk; City of Toronto Archives; City of Toronto Urban Affairs Library; City of Ottawa Elections Officer; City of Montreal Archives.

Average turnout in the 1990s for these seven cities was 43.2 percent. This is somewhat higher than the figure that Kushner and his colleagues obtained for Ontario cities with populations of over 100,000 in 1994, but it is still low enough to be a cause for concern. The majority of eligible voters in some of Canada's largest cities are simply not voting. If the association between the size of a municipality and voter turnout that Kushner and his colleagues observed in Ontario holds more generally, the trend toward municipal mergers bodes ill for municipal turnout (Kushner, Siegel, and Stanwick 1997). It is too early to see the effects of the municipal mergers in Toronto (1998), Ottawa (2001), and Montreal (2001), but Kushner and his colleagues' findings imply that larger municipalities may mean lower voter turnout in the long run. Oliver's (2000) data on municipal elections in the United States point in the same direction.

In the absence of survey data, it is impossible to say anything about who votes in municipal elections, or if age affects municipal voting in the way it affects federal voting. Unlike federal elections, voter turnout in municipal elections does not appear to have declined consistently since 1990. This raises two possibilities. Either young Canadians are not disengaging to the same degree from municipal politics, or their turnout to vote in municipal elections has always been low. Certainly, life-cycle effects could be even stronger at the municipal level, but in the absence of direct evidence, that interpretation remains speculative.

How Active Are Canadians in Election Campaigns?

As we noted above, turnout in federal elections might increase if political parties intensified their efforts to contact voters. This presupposes, though, that there is a "reserve army" of supporters available to stuff envelopes and go door to door. The stark fact is, however, that fewer than one Canadian in ten did *anything* to help a party or candidate during the 2000 federal election campaign, where "help" included such easy activities as putting a sticker on their car or a sign in their yard, as well as more demanding activities like going to a rally or working for a candidate.

Russell Dalton and his colleagues (Dalton, McAllister, and Wattenberg 2000, 57-9) have documented a generally declining trend in election campaign involvement in Australia, Canada, the United States, and six European countries. The only exception is the Netherlands, where there was no discernible trend between 1972 and 1989 in the number of campaign activities in which Dutch citizens engage. The international comparison reveals that the decline in attendance at election meetings has been steepest in Canada, followed at some distance by Switzerland. Meanwhile, the decline in working for a political party (or candidate) has been most evident in Switzerland, but Canada ranks second, just ahead of Australia. Canada also ranks behind Switzerland when it comes to the drop-off in the percentage of people who report that they have tried to convince others how to vote. Switzerland and Canada are the only two countries in which this question has been asked across time. However, trends in the percentage of people who have talked to friends about the vote in some of the other countries suggest that the decline in proselytizing activity has actually been quite modest in Canada.

Steven Rosenstone and John Hansen (1993) argue that the decline in citizens' campaign involvement is related to the changing nature of election campaigns. Political parties once relied heavily on door-to-door canvassing and campaign rallies, but now their campaigns are much more focused on the media. Public relations consultants, pollsters, advertising agencies, and media specialists have replaced the party volunteers who licked envelopes and canvassed their neighbours. Professionalized campaigns offer fewer opportunities for citizen involvement, and fewer citizens involved in party work make it harder to mount effective grassroots campaigns.

Who Are the Campaign Activists?

Given the small number of Canadians who helped out a party or candidate in any way during the 2000 campaign, it is difficult to use the survey data to say much about who these people were. However, some characteristics do stand out. The first is age. Campaign activists are disproportionately drawn from the ranks of older Canadians, born before 1945: 12 percent of pre-baby boomers had helped on a campaign compared with 9 percent of Canadians in general. This age profile is worrying because it implies that the pool of campaign activists may shrink through generational replacement. On a more positive note, members of visible minorities were more likely (13 percent) than average to have helped out during the campaign, and they constitute a growing, though still small, portion of the population.

Region of residence also seems to affect campaign activism. Campaign activists were much more numerous in Ontario (13 percent) than in Quebec (3 percent). Surprisingly, though, rural Canadians were no more likely to have helped out in the 2000 campaign than city-dwellers. Sex, household income, and education also made little difference, though university graduates were a little more likely to have been involved in some way.

How Many Canadians Are Joining Political Parties?

According to Schattschneider (1942, 1), "Modern democracy is unthinkable save in terms of political parties." In electoral democracies, political parties are the key intermediary organizations linking citizens to the state. Unlike other intermediary organizations, parties do not merely articulate societal interests, but also aggregate them into broad-ranging proposals for governing the country. This linkage function presumes a broad-based party membership. However, the increasingly common pattern in advanced industrial democracies is the emergence of "parties without partisans" (Dalton and Wattenberg 2002).

It is frustratingly difficult to determine whether Canada fits the picture of declining party membership. In contrast to electoral turnout, there is no official source of information on membership in political parties in Canada, which in itself suggests that cultivating a mass membership has not been a priority for Canadian parties over the years (Cross 2004). Instead, we have to rely on responses to survey questions to estimate how many Canadians have belonged to a political party. Surveys results typically overstate the rate of membership in political parties for two reasons. First, the people who are the least likely to be party members – those who know little and care less about politics – are also the least likely to respond to a survey about politics. Second, it is difficult to ascertain exactly how people interpret the notion of being a party member. A citizen who carries a party membership card obviously meets the basic criterion. But some loyal partisans may also think of themselves as belonging to "their" party even though they have never taken out a formal membership.

The 2000 Canadian Election Study asked Canadians whether they had *ever* belonged to a political party. The responses indicate that almost one Canadian in five has been a member of a political party at some point. This is similar to the figures obtained in surveys conducted on behalf of the Institute for Research on Public Policy (16 percent) in the spring of 2000 (Howe and Northrup 2000) and for the Royal Commission on Electoral Reform and Party Financing (Lortie Commission, 18 percent) ten years earlier (Blais and Gidengil 1991).

Data from the World Values Surveys provide some sense of where Canada ranks in terms of party membership. Rather than asking people whether they have ever belonged to a political party, the World Values Surveys ask people whether they are an active member, an inactive member, or not a member of a political party. According to the 1990 World Values Surveys, Canada was at the median for the seventeen Anglo-American, Nordic, and West European democracies: almost 8 percent of Canadians said that they were members. About half of these members fell into the active category. Canada ranked just ahead of the former West Germany and well ahead of Spain, France, and Ireland. On the other hand, Canada lagged well behind Norway,

Finland, the United States, and Iceland, which all had close to double Canada's rate. Ten years earlier, the figure for Canada stood at just over 6 percent, suggesting that, if anything, party membership had grown a little during the 1980s. Canada was not part of the 1995 World Values Surveys so it is not possible to determine whether the collapse of the Progressive Conservative Party in 1993 and the advent of two new political parties – the Reform Party (later the Canadian Alliance) and the Bloc Québécois – had any impact on levels of party membership.

Who Belongs to Political Parties?

To judge by the regional breakdowns, the tectonic shifts in the federal party system have had little effect on party membership in Canada. According to the 2000 Canadian Election Study, Quebeckers (22 percent) and Westerners (22 percent) are much more likely to have belonged to a political party than Atlantic Canadians (15 percent) or Ontarians (14 percent). Ten years earlier, the Lortie Commission survey revealed a surprisingly similar picture: Quebeckers (24 percent) and Westerners (21 percent) were much more likely to say that they had been a member of a political party at some point in their lives than either Atlantic Canadians (13 percent) or Ontarians (12 percent) (Blais and Gidengil 1991). These regional differences are not simply a function of differences in the social background of the regions' residents; they reflect differences in the nature of party politics and political traditions in different parts of the country. The Parti Québécois, for example, has been Canada's closest approximation of a mass-membership party, and it has relied heavily on the financial support of its dues-paying members (Angell 1987). In addition to Quebeckers, residents of Saskatchewan (32 percent) and Alberta (23 percent) are particularly likely to report that they have belonged to a political party at some time in their lives.

Regardless of their region of residence, rural Canadians (24 percent) are more likely to have been party members than city-dwellers (17 percent). That finding holds after differences in social background are taken into account; the implication is that the rural milieu encourages people to become involved in party politics. Conversely, being born outside Canada seems to depress party membership. Only 13 percent of people who are not Canadian by birth say that they have belonged to a political party. Recent arrivals have had less opportunity to take up party membership, but in fact the differences between those born in Canada and others shrink only for those who have lived in Canada for many years. Race, by contrast, makes little difference. Rates of party membership are not significantly different for members of visible minorities.

Belonging to a political party is a fairly demanding form of political activity. Party membership not only entails a time commitment, it also puts a premium on the possession of cognitive skills. As Norris points out (2002, ch. 7), common branch activities include "discussing local issues and party policies, chairing or writing minutes for branch meetings, drafting newsletters or press releases, selecting candidates, attending conferences, and arranging local fund-raising events." Not surprisingly, then, university-educated Canadians are significantly more likely (25 percent) to have been members of a political party. Only university education, though, seems to make a difference. Rates of party membership among those with less than a bachelor's degree are quite similar.

Party members are disproportionately drawn from the ranks of affluent Canadians. Sixteen percent of Canadians with incomes in the bottom 20 percent of households have belonged to a political party at some time in their lives, compared with 24 percent of those with household incomes in the top 20 percent. One reason poorer Canadians are less likely to have been party members is that they typically have less formal schooling. This is not the whole story, though. Something about being poor discourages membership in a political party. Poorer Canadians are less likely to believe that the political system is responsive and they are also less likely to have much interest in politics.

What really differentiates party members is their age profile. Party membership rises from a low of 5 percent among those born since

1970 to a high of 28 percent among those born before 1945. With the data at hand, it is difficult to determine whether this is simply a life-cycle effect or a generational effect. Just as people are more likely to vote as they move from their twenties to their thirties to their forties, so they are more likely to join a political party. The reasons are similar, and they relate to settling down and becoming part of the community. We do not know whether today's young Canadians are less likely to have belonged to a political party than their parents were when they were the same age. At the time of the Lortie Commission survey in 1990, however, almost twice as many eighteen-to-thirty-year-olds, nearly 10 percent, said that they had been party members (Blais and Gidengil 1991). Another possible indication of generational change is the fact that powerful age-group effects persisted in 2000, even when a variety of factors associated with life cycle, such as marital status, having children, and employment status, were taken into account.

As we have seen, there is little sign of a gender gap in turnout to vote, even though women tend to be less interested in politics. Religiosity and sense of duty, it seems, help motivate some women to vote despite their lack of interest. When it comes to more demanding forms of political participation, however, a gender gap does begin to appear. According to the 2000 Canadian Election Study, men (20 percent) are more likely than women (17 percent) to have been a member of a political party at some time in their lives. This gap appears to be stable; ten years earlier, the Canada-wide survey conducted on behalf of the Lortie Commission found a similar 3 point gap. Still, the difference between women and men is rather modest. To put the gap in perspective, pooling data from the World Values Surveys for fifty-nine countries, Norris (2002, ch. 7) found a difference of over 5 points overall in rates of party membership for women and men in the early to mid-1990s. Moreover, unlike the gap observed by Norris, the difference between Canadian men and women can be explained by differences in educational attainment, income, and other personal characteristics. Still, the larger point remains that party members are disproportionately male. Interestingly, when they did belong to a political party, women (82 percent) were more likely than men (75 percent) to say that they had attended meetings or spent time canvassing for the party or helping the party get things done (Howe and Northrup 2000).

How Many Canadian Are Joining Interest Groups?

One reason so few Canadians have ever belonged to a political party is that they do not see political parties as effective vehicles. The 2000 Canadian Election Study asked Canadians which was the more effective way of working for change: joining a political party or joining an interest group. The answer was joining an interest group by a margin of three to one (61 percent versus 20 percent). Aside from the fact that women (16 percent) were even less likely than men (24 percent) to opt for joining a political party, people's social background characteristics made surprisingly little difference: young or old, high school dropouts or university graduates, rich or poor, Canadians chose interest groups over political parties by a margin of two or three to one. At the same time, though, there is no indication that Canadians are flocking to join interest groups. On the contrary, fewer Canadians have actually belonged to interest groups than to political parties.

Reliable information on the number of Canadians who belong to interest groups is even harder to find than an accurate count of party members (see Young and Everitt 2004). Again, we have to rely on survey data, and again, we need to bear in mind that people may be vague about the concept of belonging to an interest group. The 2000 Canadian Election Study asked Canadians whether they had ever been "a member of an interest group that worked for change on a particular social or political issue." Canadians seem even less likely to have belonged to an interest group (11 percent) than they are to have belonged to a political party (18 percent). The IRPP survey in spring 2000 reported a very similar figure for interest group membership (12 percent). Because the same question was not asked in previous surveys it is not possible to tell if Canadians have become more or less enthusiastic about joining interest groups. According to the IRPP survey, most of the people who have belonged to an interest group at some time in their lives were active members: only one in ten indicated that they had not attended meetings or spent time trying to get things done.

Who Belongs to Interest Groups?

Like belonging to a political party, belonging to an interest group requires cognitive skills. So it comes as no surprise that university graduates are significantly more likely (20 percent) to have belonged to an interest group at some time in their lives. Education also explains why affluent Canadians are twice as likely (16 percent) to have been interest group members as poorer Canadians (8 percent). Indeed, when educational differences are taken into account, income makes little difference to the likelihood of belonging to an interest group. Nonetheless, the fact remains that affluent and well-educated Canadians are overrepresented in the membership rolls of interest groups.

In contrast to party membership, where people live makes little difference. Urban Canadians are as likely to have belonged to an interest group as rural Canadians. And while Atlantic Canadians are less likely to be involved in interest groups, this can mostly be accounted for by differences in educational attainment and material circumstances. As we have seen, people who were born outside Canada are less likely to have been party members. In the case of interest groups, though, what matters is not place of birth, but race: members of visible minorities are less likely to have belonged to an interest group. This holds true even when other social background characteristics such as income and education are taken into account. In an important sense, then, interest groups are less representative of Canada's diversity than are political parties.

Although women were a little less likely to have been party members than men, there is no gender gap when it comes to membership in interest groups. Even though fewer women are university graduates (though this is changing), women are as likely as men to have belonged at some point in their lives to an interest group that was working for political or social change.

Age is also a factor. People born before 1945 are almost twice as likely (13 percent) as those born since 1970 (7 percent) to have belonged to an interest group. The opportunity to have *ever* belonged to an interest group – or a political party – is, of course, partly a function of age. Intriguingly, however, age has less impact on interest group membership than on membership in a political party. People born before 1945 were more than five times as likely (28 percent) to have been party members as those born since 1970 (5 percent), but only twice as likely to have belonged to an interest group. And only among the youngest age group are people at least as likely to have belonged to an interest group as to a political party. Still, there are reasons to be cautious about reading too much into these figures. The larger point is that so few young Canadians have ever belonged to either an interest group or a political party.

Interest groups are sometimes assumed to compete with political parties for members. According to the Royal Commission on Electoral Reform and Party Financing (cited in Howe and Northrup 2000, 33-4), for example, "Many political activists, who previously would have pursued their public policy interests through a political party, now participate in advocacy and interest groups." Proponents of interest groups see membership as offering a more meaningful form of political engagement. Critics, meanwhile, bemoan the narrow scope of interest group initiatives, contrasting them unfavourably with the efforts of political parties to build broader coalitions. But in important respects, the profiles of party members and interest group members are quite similar, which suggests that interest groups and political parties might in fact be complementary rather than competing forms of involvement in politics. Howe and Northrup (2000) reach a similar conclusion, based on the data that they collected for the IRPP.

The Canadian Election Survey data seem to support this notion. Twenty-two percent of people who have belonged to a political party have also belonged to an interest group, compared with only 8 percent of those who have never been party members. Meanwhile, 38 percent of people who have been members of an interest group at some time in their lives have also been members of a political party, compared with only 16 percent of those who have never belonged to an interest group. This pattern holds for younger and older Canadians alike. Indeed, it actually holds more strongly for those born since 1970: young Canadians who have been members of an interest group are almost five times as likely (19 percent) to have belonged to a political party as nonmembers (4 percent), while those who have belonged to a political party are four times as likely (24 percent) to have been members of an interest group as those who have not been party members (6 percent). People in general are much more likely to belong to *either* a political party *or* an interest group than they are to belong to both, but those who belong to one are much more likely than the population at large to belong to the other.

Are Canadians Turning to Political Protest?

Regardless of their social background and personal situation, Canadians think that joining an interest group is a better way of achieving change than joining a political party. Even so, social background is relevant to Canadians' opinions about the most effective way to work for change; it made a significant difference to their views about whether joining either a political party or an interest group would be of any use. Fully a quarter of those who left school without a high school diploma either did not know or said that neither would be effective, compared with fewer than one in ten university graduates. Similarly, people from low-income households were much more likely (23 percent) than their affluent counterparts (9 percent) to respond that they did not know or could not tell. Members of visible minorities were also more likely (23 percent) than average not to know or not to see membership in either political parties or interest groups as an effective way of working for change. Surprisingly, though, those who were born before 1945 were the most likely (19 percent) to respond the same way, not those born since 1970 (13 percent). Only just over half of the older age group opted for interest groups, while almost a quarter chose political parties.

The fact that so many Canadians apparently see neither political parties nor interest groups as effective vehicles of change raises the question of whether they are turning to other, more meaningful forms of political involvement. So, too, does the fact that only a minority of Canadians have actually been members of a political party or an interest group. After all, belonging to political parties or interest groups is a very traditional mode of political involvement. Canadians could be turning to less conventional political activities instead.

The 2000 Canadian Election Study presented respondents with a list of political actions that people can take and asked them to indicate which actions they themselves either had taken or might take. The choices were signing a petition, joining in a boycott, attending a lawful demonstration, joining an illegal strike, and occupying a building or factory. The responses suggest that a majority of Canadians (84 percent) have signed a petition on at least one occasion, and most of those who have not would certainly consider doing so (see Figure 5.6).

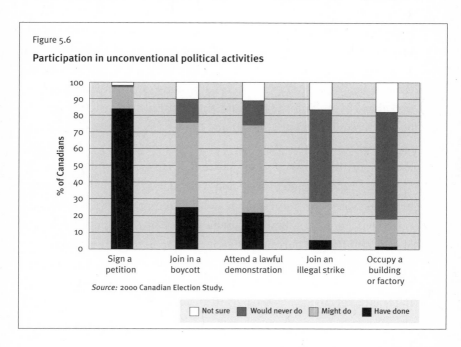

Figure 5.6

Participation in unconventional political activities

Source: 2000 Canadian Election Study.

Not sure   Would never do   Might do   Have done

How Much Do Canadians Participate in Politics?

On the other hand, only one in four have joined in a boycott and fewer still have attended a lawful demonstration. In both cases, a sizable minority (14 or 15 percent) indicated that they would never take part in such activities. Few Canadians report engaging in unlawful forms of protest: just 6 percent of respondents indicated that they had joined an illegal strike at some time and a mere 2 percent have occupied a building or factory. The majority of Canadians (55 percent and 64 percent respectively) say that they would never take such actions. Only 15 percent of Canadians have never taken part in any of these protest activities. Similar numbers have participated in three or more of the different protest activities. One in five Canadians have joined in two protest activities, while one in two have participated in only one, typically signing a petition.

The 1990 World Values Surveys help to place these Canadian findings in an international context. Precisely where Canada ranks among established democracies depends very much on the activity in question. Canada (77 percent) actually topped the list when it came to signing petitions, ahead of Britain, Sweden, and the United States and well above the median, which was in the low fifties. Canada (22 percent) also ranked first for joining in boycotts, just ahead of Iceland and the United States, and well above the median of 12 percent. For more assertive acts, though, Canada slips down the list. At 21 percent, Canada was right at the median for attending lawful demonstrations, well ahead of Finland and Britain (14 percent) and Austria (10 percent), but far behind Italy (36 percent) and France (33 percent). Norwegians (24 percent) and Danes (17 percent) were the most likely to have taken part in an illegal strike. At 7 percent, Canada was just above the median, slightly ahead of Italy and Iceland, but well ahead of the former West Germany, Switzerland, and the Netherlands (2 percent) and Austria (1 percent). Finally, Canada (3 percent) ranked well behind France and Italy (8 percent) when it came to occupying a building or factory, but fourth overall. Most countries were clustered around the median of 2 percent. At less than 1 percent, Austrians and Swedes were the least likely to have taken part in an occupation.

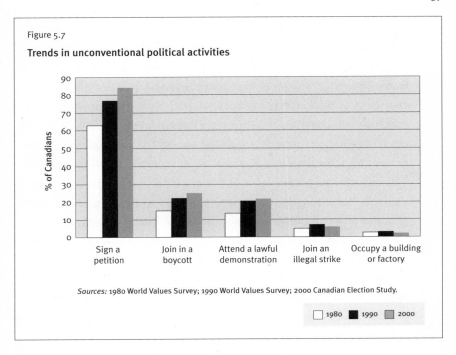

Figure 5.7

Trends in unconventional political activities

Sources: 1980 World Values Survey; 1990 World Values Survey; 2000 Canadian Election Study.

☐ 1980 ■ 1990 ▨ 2000

Participation in protest activities appears to have increased over the past twenty years (see Figure 5.7). Between 1980 and 2000, the percentage of Canadians who have signed a petition jumped by over 20 points. Meanwhile, joining in a boycott was up 10 points, while attending a lawful demonstration was up 8 points. There has been little change, however, in the percentage joining an illegal strike or occupying a building or factory. These unlawful acts of protest remain the preserve of a very small minority.

The 1980 and 1990 World Values Surveys yield a similar picture. Between 1980 and 1990, signing petitions was up by an average of 11 points for our comparison group of established democracies, while joining in boycotts grew by an average of 4 points and attending lawful demonstrations by an average of 6 points. By contrast, participation in illegal strikes grew by only 2 points on average and there was no change at all in the majority of these countries when it came to more dramatic activities such as occupying a building or factory.

Who Joins in Protest Activities?

The fact that participation in lawful protest activities increased across these countries suggests that some general process of structural change is at work. Nevitte (1996) has pointed to the transformations that have accompanied the shift from industrial to postindustrial society. These include greatly enhanced access to higher education, the growth of a "new middle class" of professionals, semiprofessionals, and technocrats in the wake of the expansion of the tertiary sector, and the "information revolution" that has accompanied the emergence of new communication technologies. These structural changes have been paralleled by significant value shifts. The key reference point here is Inglehart's (1971; 1990) thesis about the rise of postmaterialist values. Spared the traumas of the Depression and world war, he argues, many of those born since 1945 have been able to take their physical and economic security more or less for granted. As a consequence, they have been able to look beyond their material needs and to seek gratification of their need for self-actualization. Taken together, these structural and cultural shifts have led to the emergence of increasing numbers of citizens who have the cognitive skills, the access to information, and the motivation to pursue more autonomous forms of political involvement.

Indeed, people's propensity to engage in protest activities shows a clear generational difference. Members of the baby boom generation, born between 1945 and 1959, are much more likely to have participated in various kinds of protest activity. Nine in ten have signed a petition, one in three have joined in a boycott, more than one in four have attended a lawful demonstration, and almost one in ten have taken part in an illegal strike at some time in their lives. One baby boomer in five has taken part in at least three different types of protest activity, compared with only one in ten of the generation born before 1945. The baby boomers are the postmaterialist generation par excellence, the first to grow to adulthood in the relative affluence that characterized the postwar period. A similar pattern appears internationally: protest activists are most likely to be found among the middle-aged (Norris 2002).

Interestingly, in Canada, the generation born since 1970 ranks second when it comes to involvement in three or more different protest activities. True, this is also the generation whose members are the most likely (22 percent) to have engaged in no protest activities whatsoever, but there is also a core of young Canadians who are seeking to effect change by engaging in protest activities. The question is, have these young Canadians turned their back on more conventional means of making their voices heard? It seems not. Young Canadians who have engaged in three or more different protest activities are *more* likely than other members of their generation to belong to a political party (9 percent) or to an interest group (26 percent). This phenomenon applies to all age groups; people who have engaged in protest activities of any kind are more likely to have belonged to a political party or an interest group than the population at large.

Unsurprisingly, it is often the *same* Canadians who are joining political parties, joining interest groups, and engaging in various forms of protest. The common denominator is higher education. Almost a third of university-educated Canadians have joined in a boycott or attended a lawful demonstration, and almost one university graduate in five has taken part in at least three different protest activities. Meanwhile, Canadians whose education ended without a high school diploma are the least likely to have engaged in any protest activities. They rank lowest on signing petitions (76 percent), joining in boycotts (19 percent), and attending lawful demonstrations (12 percent), though they are about as likely as Canadians in general to have been involved in an illegal strike (6 percent). These differences persist even after other social background characteristics are taken into account. Political awareness is part of the story. The less education people have, the less likely they are to be aware of what is going on, and people who are less aware are less likely to become involved in protest activities. Engaging in protest activities also seems to require cognitive skills.

This helps to explain why poorer Canadians are less likely to have engaged in various forms of protest. This is true of signing petitions (76 percent), joining in boycotts (19 percent), attending lawful demonstrations (14 percent), and taking part in illegal strikes (3 percent). Protest activities do not seem to provide the poor with an alternative means of making their voices heard. Like party politics and interest group politics, protest politics tends to be the preserve of those who are comfortably off. This represents a profound change from the days when "protest was concentrated among the socially disadvantaged, repressed minorities or groups that were alienated from the established political order. Unconventional political action was an outlet for groups that lacked access to politics through conventional participation channels" (Dalton 2002, 59).

Protest politics also tends to be the preserve of the Canadian born, especially those of European ancestry. Among those of non-European ancestry, fully one-third have not taken part in any form of protest activity. The same is true of more than a quarter of those born outside Canada. Many of them may have come from countries where protest activities are banned, which may partly explain their lower participation.

Region of residence generally has only a modest effect on the propensity to engage in protest activities. Westerners are less likely than residents of other regions to have attended a lawful demonstration (17 percent) or taken part in an illegal strike (3 percent), while Quebeckers are more likely to have participated in an illegal strike (10 percent) or occupied a building or factory (6 percent). Beyond this, the regional differences are minimal. Rural and urban Canadians also have very similar levels of involvement in the various forms of protest activity.

Public sector employees and people from union households are particularly likely to have been involved in protest activities. This is true of joining in boycotts, attending lawful demonstrations, and taking part in illegal strikes, as well as signing petitions. Meanwhile, religiosity seems to depress protest activity, especially when it comes to joining in boycotts and attending lawful demonstrations. Finally, there is one significant sex difference: women (88 percent) are more likely than men (81 percent) to have signed a petition. In general, though, involvement in protest activities is very similar for women and men alike.

When middle-aged, well-educated, and relatively affluent Canadians are the most likely to have taken part in protest activities, it is clear that "protest has gone from margin to mainstream" (Norris 2002, 201). In Canada, as in other established democracies, the profile of protest activists has "normalized" (Van Aelst and Walgrave 2001). Signing petitions, joining in boycotts, and attending lawful demonstrations are now fairly mainstream ways of voicing concerns and expressing dissent. However, participating in illegal strikes and occupying buildings and factories remain beyond the realm of acceptable political behaviour.

Discussion

This survey of political participation in Canada provides little cause for celebrating the state of democratic citizenship in Canada. Turnout in federal elections is low by international standards and has plummeted in the three most recent elections. Few Canadians take an active part in election campaigns and their numbers appear to be dwindling. Canadians are skeptical about the value of joining political parties and relatively few have ever been party members. Even fewer have ever belonged to an interest group.

Certainly, more Canadians than ever before are engaging in various forms of political protest, and Canada actually ranks first among advanced industrial democracies when it comes to signing petitions and joining in boycotts. But signing a petition requires little time or effort, and joining in a boycott may require none whatsoever. Declining to buy a particular brand of sneakers or line of clothing is a passive (though potentially quite influential) form of protest. And Canadians are not much more likely to have joined in a boycott than they are to have belonged to a political party.

The low level of political participation is not the only cause for concern. Even more disconcerting is the profile of those who participate. Party members, for example, are disproportionately white, male, affluent, and advancing in years. Indeed, whatever mode of participation we look at, there is a recurring pattern: the young, the less educated, and the poor are less likely to be involved.

The decline in turnout in federal elections on the part of young, less educated Canadians is particularly startling. And there is little indication that these young Canadians are turning to other forms of political engagement. To be sure, a core of young Canadians are very active politically, but they are drawn disproportionately from the ranks of the university educated. For this activist group, as for their older counterparts, newer forms of political engagement are not so much supplanting more traditional forms as providing additional avenues of expression.

As Dalton (2002) observes, the mainstreaming of protest politics is actually widening the participation gap. In Canada, as in other advanced industrial democracies, the affluent and the highly educated are the most likely to sign petitions, join in boycotts, and attend lawful demonstrations, just as they are more likely to vote, to become members of political parties, and to join interest groups. They have voice, and those with voice are more likely to be heard. It may be tempting to blame lack of political participation on lack of interest and motivation, but these all have deeper roots in poverty, lack of literacy skills, and unrepresentative institutions.

Chapter 5

- Turnout in federal elections has dropped 14 percentage points since 1988. The drop is largely the result of generational replacement.
- Fewer than one Canadian in ten takes an active part in election campaigns.
- Fewer than one Canadian in five has ever belonged to a political party.
- Only about one Canadian in ten has ever belonged to an interest group.
- Five Canadians in six have signed a petition, but only one in four has ever joined in a boycott.
- Very few Canadians have joined in an illegal strike or occupied a building or factory, and a majority of Canadians say they would never engage in such activities.
- The young, the less educated, and the less affluent are the least likely to be involved in any form of political activity.

6   HOW CIVIC-MINDED ARE CANADIANS?

So far, the focus has been on Canadians' involvement in politics and government. In this chapter, the focus broadens to examine Canadians' involvement in the community at large. A long tradition in democratic theory, going back to Alexis de Tocqueville and John Stuart Mill, links democratic health to the vitality of civil society. Building on this tradition, James Coleman (1988), Robert Putnam (2000) and others have argued powerfully that a healthy democracy requires an adequate stock of "social capital." According to Putnam, "social capital refers to connections among individuals – social networks and the norms of reciprocity and trustworthiness that arise from them" (p. 19). The central idea is that "networks of community engagement foster sturdy norms of reciprocity" (p. 20). As such, they encourage a quality that is crucial to a well-functioning democracy, namely "the willingness of opposing sides in a democratic debate to agree on the ground rules for seeking mutual accommodation after sufficient discussion, even (or especially) when they don't agree on what is to be done" (p. 340).

At a less lofty level, community involvement can provide people with a way of making their needs and interests known to public officials. When people become active in voluntary associations, "their individual and otherwise quiet voices multiply and are amplified" (Putnam 2000, 338). Associational involvement is also said to encourage political discussion and the exchange of political information. In addition to these "external" effects, Putnam points to the "internal" effects of community involvement on those who take an active part. These benefits range from inculcating civic virtues like political engagement, trustworthiness and trust in others, and reciprocity to imparting social and civic skills that facilitate participation in public affairs.

This may be too rosy a view, however. Far from levelling the playing field by offering a voice to the poor and uneducated, associational activity may reinforce the inequalities that characterize participation in public affairs. Active membership in a voluntary association pre-supposes that a person possesses basic literacy skills and verbal fluency. It also requires time and possibly social connections. So it could well be that "associational ties benefit those who are best equipped by nature or circumstance to organize and make their voices heard" (Putnam 2000, 340).

Therefore we cannot simply look at how active Canadians are in voluntary associations; we also need to pay close attention to *who* is active. Does associational activity offer people at the political margins a way to have more influence over public affairs, or does it reproduce existing inequalities in the political sphere? Are people who are active in voluntary organizations more active in politics as well? Are they more informed about politics, and do they discuss politics more often? What about other indicators of social capital, like volunteerism, altruism, and philanthropy? How many Canadians are donating to worthy causes or volunteering their time to help others?

How Many Canadians Are Active in Voluntary Associations?

One of Putnam's (2000, 336) core arguments is that "the health of our *public* institutions depends, at least in part, on widespread participation in *private* voluntary groups – those networks of civic engagement that embody social capital." By this criterion, Canadian democracy qualifies as relatively healthy. The 2000 Canadian Election Study

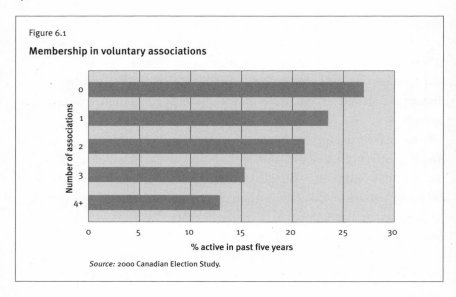

Figure 6.1

Membership in voluntary associations

Source: 2000 Canadian Election Study.

found that the average Canadian had been active in one or two associations over the past five years (see Figure 6.1). And some Canadians were very active indeed: one in eight had been active in four or more voluntary associations in the previous five years. At the other extreme, double that number had been active in none.

One way to judge whether this is a high or a low level of associational involvement is to compare Canada with other established Western democracies. The World Values Surveys have data on membership in voluntary organizations for sixteen North American, Nordic, and West European democracies. The 1990 surveys are the most recent to include Canada. Respondents were first asked whether they belonged to any of the listed types of organization and then whether they did unpaid work for any of them. On the basis of their responses, they were classified as active members, inactive members, and nonmembers. We focus on active members. As Putnam (2000, 58) notes, "What really matters from the point of view of social capital and civic engagement is not merely nominal membership, but active and involved membership." The organizations on the list were church or religious organization, sport or recreation organization, art, music or educational organization, labour union, environmental organization, professional association, charitable organization, and any other voluntary organization. Political party was also on the list, but we have not included responses to that option in our counts.

Canadians proved to be much more active in civic life than average. Thirty-seven percent were active members of at least one voluntary organization, which was well above the median (25 percent). Canada ranked third, behind the United States and Finland and just ahead of Sweden and Norway. Sixteen percent of Canadians were active in two or more organizations. This put Canada at the top of the list, tied with the United States and Finland. The median was 8 percent.

In the 2000 Canadian Election Study, the most commonly reported type of civic engagement was membership in a community service group (see Figure 6.2). Almost half of those surveyed indicated that they had been active in a community service group during the past five years. A third had been active in religious organizations or sports associations and a quarter had been active in a professional association.

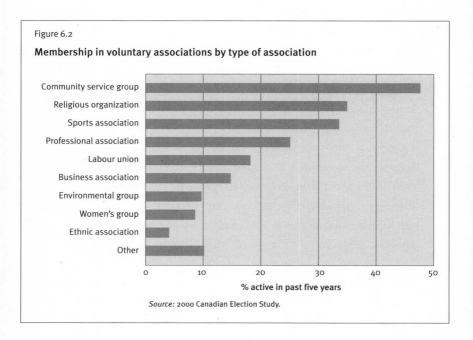

Figure 6.2

Membership in voluntary associations by type of association

% active in past five years

Source: 2000 Canadian Election Study.

Again, we can use data from the 1990 World Values Surveys to see how Canada compares in terms of each type of associational involvement. Although the list of voluntary associations differs somewhat from the Canadian Election Study, for those organizations that were common to both studies, the rankings were quite similar. According to the 1990 World Values Surveys, the most common form of involvement for Canadians (among those listed) was in religious organizations. Fifteen percent indicated that they were currently active members of a church or religious organization. This put Canada well ahead of the Netherlands (9 percent), which ranked next, but far behind the United States (29 percent). North Americans are clearly much more involved in religious organizations than West Europeans or Scandinavians. The median for the sixteen countries was only 6 percent.

Sports and recreation organizations ranked right behind church and religious organizations, but they were not as popular in Canada (12 percent) as they were in Scandinavia. The median was around 8 or 9 percent. Art, music, and educational organizations were also popular with Canadians (9 percent). Canada ranked in the top three for this type of activity, just behind the Netherlands and the United States, and well above the median for the sixteen countries, which was around 5 percent. Canada also ranked third for active membership in professional associations (5 percent), just behind Finland and the United States. Relatively few Canadians (4 percent) were active in environmental organizations, but they were numerous enough to put Canada in top spot, just ahead of the United States and Finland. Canada ranked fourth for active membership in labour unions (4 percent), behind Finland, Sweden, and Norway, but only sixth for involvement in charitable organizations (6 percent). Active membership in charitable organizations was most frequent in Iceland, the Netherlands, and Finland.

The World Values Surveys can also help us to see how patterns of civic activity have changed. According to the 1980 World Values Surveys, only a quarter of Canadians were active members of at least one voluntary organization. By 1990, this figure had jumped to well over a third. Most of the established democracies, except Britain and Spain, witnessed increases over the same period, ranging from 5 percentage points in Ireland and Belgium to 23 percentage points in Finland. At 11 points, the Canadian increase was very close to the median of 12 points for the fifteen countries for which cross-time data are available. This general trend toward increased associational activity is understandable: the rise in educational levels in Western democracies means that more citizens have the cognitive skills and resources that encourage active involvement in voluntary associations.

Who Belongs to Voluntary Associations?

As Chapter 5 showed, the young, the poor, and those with lower levels of formal education are less likely to participate in politics. Do community organizations provide an alternative way for the disengaged to be active in public life? The answer is clear: these same Canadians are also less likely to be actively involved in voluntary organizations (see Figure 6.3).

Canadians born since 1970 are significantly less likely than Canadians in their thirties to have been active in one or more voluntary associations; the difference is almost 10 points, according to the 2000 Canadian Election Study. Associational involvement peaks among baby boomers and then begins to fall off among older Canadians. It is tempting to attribute this pattern to life cycle. Maybe people in their thirties are more involved in voluntary organizations than younger people because they have begun to put roots down in the community. If they are parents, for example, their children's activities may lead them to become involved in sports groups or other recreation groups. Similarly, having school-age children may lead to involvement in a parent-teacher association or other school-related group. People in this age group are also more likely to be settled into a steady pattern of employment, leading them to become active in their union, professional association, or business association. As people move into their forties and fifties, family and other responsibilities will make fewer

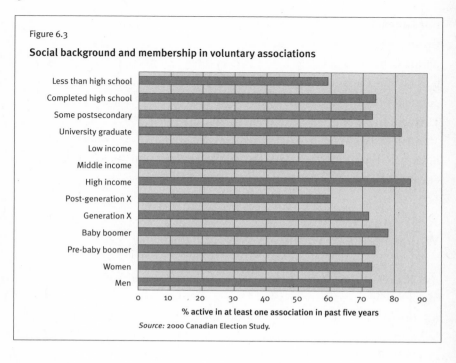

Figure 6.3

Social background and membership in voluntary associations

% active in at least one association in past five years

Source: 2000 Canadian Election Study.

demands on their time and energy, leaving more scope for involvement in voluntary associations. This involvement will begin to taper off, though, as old age sets in.

Plausible as these life-cycle effects are, we cannot rule out the possibility of generational differences. Unfortunately, we do not have the data to sort out which matters more, life cycle or generation. Age differences in involvement in voluntary associations are nothing new. The 1968 and 1984 Canadian Election Studies both included questions about membership in voluntary associations. In 1968 there was a 7 point gap between people in their thirties and those aged thirty or less. In 1984 the gap was 5 points. The implication that there is an important life-cycle aspect to the age differences is supported by age differences in the *type* of associational involvement. For example, Canadians born since 1970 are almost twice as likely (40 percent) as Canadians born before 1945 (22 percent) to have been active in a sports association in the past five years. The same applies to Canadians in their thirties (42 percent). Meanwhile, baby boomers are the most likely to have been active in a professional association (32 percent), a labour union (24 percent), or a business association (19 percent).

The fact that young Canadians are less likely to be active in at least one voluntary association casts doubt on the optimistic assumption that greater involvement in grassroots-level activities is offsetting the decline in their political participation. If young Canadians are turning to other, more meaningful forms of engagement, this should show up in membership of environmental groups. The environment is an issue of concern to young people that ranks low on the country's political agenda. Frustrated by the lack of action, young Canadians might seek to effect change by becoming actively involved in environmental groups. However, Canadians born since 1970 are no more likely (9 percent) than Canadians in general to have been active in an environmental group.

Material circumstances clearly have an impact on people's involvement in voluntary associations. The better off are significantly more likely to have been active in at least one voluntary organization over the past five years. According to the 2000 Canadian Election Study, the gap between people with household incomes in the top 20 percent and the bottom 20 percent is over 20 points. This income gap is sizeable, but it is smaller than the international average according to both the 1980 and 1990 World Values Surveys. These same surveys indicate that the income gap in associational involvement in Canada has grown wider since 1980, as it has in the majority of established Western democracies.

Understandably, people who are preoccupied with making ends meet may simply have little energy left over to participate in voluntary associations. But there is more to it than the pressures of financial worry. Patterns of employment also make for differences in associational activity. Predictably, affluent people are far more likely to be active in a professional association (39 percent) or a business association (29 percent), while labour union involvement is most common among people in the medium (24 percent) to medium-high (27 percent) income categories.

In other types of associations, such as environmental groups and religious organizations, the least affluent are as active as other Canadians. And the least affluent are actually the most likely (12 percent) to have been active in a women's group. Interestingly, better-off Canadians are the most likely to have been active in an ethnic association. This is also the case for sports associations. People with household incomes in the top 20 percent are more than twice as likely (47 percent) as those in the bottom 20 percent (18 percent) to have been active in a sports association in the past five years.

Education is a factor, too. The more education people have, the more likely they are to have been active in one or more associations. The World Values Surveys reveal a similar pattern across most advanced industrial states. In 1990 the gap between university graduates and high school dropouts in Canada was just below the median for the sixteen countries for which figures are available. However, the most important divide was not between those who had a university education and those who did not, but between those who had completed high school and those who had not. The 2000 Canadian Election Study told a similar story: the gap was a full 15 points. It was largest for sports associations and community service groups.

The impact of education on voluntary association membership is independent of household income. This suggests that a lack of basic literacy skills or verbal fluency is inhibiting greater involvement. And of course education and occupation are related. People who lack a high school diploma are unlikely to be in occupations that encourage involvement in professional or business associations. The gap disappears when it comes to active involvement in labour unions. Similarly, having a high school diploma makes little difference to involvement with religious organizations. In fact, people who left school without a high school diploma are as likely as university graduates to have been active in these organizations.

Men and women have very similar levels of associational involvement, but they differ when it comes to the *type* of association in which they are active (see Figure 6.4). Not surprisingly, involvement in women's groups is almost wholly confined to women, but women are

Figure 6.4

Sex differences in associational activity

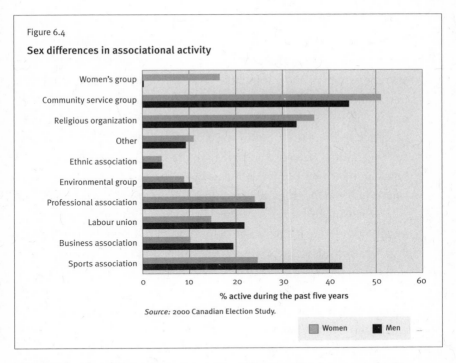

% active during the past five years

Source: 2000 Canadian Election Study.

Women   Men

also much more likely than men to have been active in a community service group or in a religious organization. Men, meanwhile, are more likely than women to have been active in work-related organizations and in sports associations.

Quebeckers are the least likely (60 percent) to have been active in at least one voluntary association over the past five years. This could be attributable to the fact that Quebeckers tend to be more secular and therefore much less likely (14 percent) to be involved in religious organizations. However, the difference persists even when we disregard involvement in religious organizations. In fact, whichever type of association we look at, Quebeckers rank last or next to last. Nova Scotia (87 percent), Manitoba (82 percent), and Saskatchewan (81 percent) have the highest levels of group involvement. The level of active involvement in voluntary associations is very similar for residents of rural and urban areas. Only after other differences in social background and province of residence are taken into account do rural Canadians appear to be more active than their urban counterparts.

How Civic-Minded Are Canadians?

People born outside Canada are generally as active in voluntary associations as other Canadians, unless they arrived in the past ten years. Recent arrivals tend to be much less involved (58 percent) than average, which is understandable given the demands of adapting to a new country. Members of visible minorities, whether born in Canada or not, are less likely (66 percent) than Canadians in general to have been active in at least one voluntary association. This remains the case even when we take account of factors such as age, education, and household income. But it is not true of every type of voluntary association. Visible minorities are just as likely as other Canadians to be active in women's groups and environmental groups, and they are much more likely (51 percent) than average to be active in religious organizations. Not surprisingly, the same applies to ethnic associations (15 percent).

Putnam's (2000, 340) concerns about the possible biases of associationalism appear to be warranted: "Social capital is self-reinforcing and benefits most those who already have a stock on which to trade." If patterns of active involvement in voluntary associations are any guide, the educated, the affluent, and the connected are the most likely to benefit from the existence of these networks of community engagement. One of the prime benefits is said to be a higher level of political engagement: active membership in voluntary associations provides opportunities to acquire information about politics and stimulates discussions about political affairs. But are people politically engaged because they are active in voluntary associations, or does political engagement encourage people to become active in the community at large? We cannot answer this question, but we can determine whether people who are active in voluntary associations are more interested and involved in politics than their social background characteristics would lead us to expect.

The answer is clearly "yes." People who are active in voluntary associations have more interest in politics, pay more attention to news about politics in the newspapers or on the radio, and engage in more political discussion than other people. The one exception to this pattern concerns the amount of attention paid to the television news, but, as noted in Chapter 2, this is the most passive way of following politics. People who are more active in voluntary associations also tend to know more about politics in general. They are more familiar with election promises and they can identify more political actors. They are also more likely to have been members of a political party or an interest group at some time in their lives and to have taken part in various forms of protest.

According to Putnam, involvement in voluntary associations also fosters social trust. Just as Putnam (2000) would predict, people who are active in voluntary associations are more likely to reject the idea that most people take advantage of others whenever they can. Again, the direction of the causal arrow, to borrow Putnam's phrase, is "as tangled as well-tossed spaghetti" (p. 137). Does active involvement in voluntary associations make people more trusting, or do trusting people get drawn into associational life? What we can say is this: people who belong to voluntary associations are more trusting than we would expect, given their social background characteristics.

Putnam emphasizes the link between social experiences and generalized trust. Have-nots, for example, are less trusting than haves: according to the 2000 Canadian Election Study only 43 percent of Canadians with household incomes in the bottom 20 percent think that most people can be trusted, compared with 68 percent of those in the top 20 percent. Similarly, people who left school without a high school diploma are much less trusting (40 percent) than university graduates (72 percent). Members of visible minorities (42 percent) and people who came to Canada as immigrants (47 percent) are also less trusting, and so are Quebeckers (40 percent). All of these differences hold after other social background characteristics are taken into account. Poorer Canadians, for example, are less trusting than we would expect, even allowing for the fact that they are more likely to have dropped out of high school. These same characteristics also seem to be associated with a lower level of involvement in voluntary associations, but none of them can explain why people who are less active in voluntary associations are also less trusting of others.

At the very least, we can say that generalized trust and active engagement in voluntary associations tend to go hand in hand. And they may very well be mutually reinforcing, as Putnam (2000) suggests. To the extent that generalized trust helps citizens to accept the give and take that necessarily accompanies democratic politics, the relatively high level of associational activity contributes to Canada's democratic health. However, we need to be mindful of the social inequalities that characterize involvement in voluntary associations (or at least some of them). Poorer Canadians, less educated Canadians, and Canadians who are less integrated into the mainstream of Canadian life reap fewer benefits from the existence of active networks of voluntary associations. Canadian democracy may be less healthy in consequence.

How Many Canadians Are Volunteering?

Like generalized trust, altruism is an important indicator of social capital. According to Putnam (2000, 116-7), though, altruism is part of the definition of social capital only if it involves doing *with* other people, as opposed to simply doing *for* other people. The embedding of altruistic acts in networks of social connection is what contributes to social capital. A report prepared by Michael Hall and his colleagues (Hall, McKeown, and Roberts 2001) summarizing key findings from the 2000 National Survey on Giving, Volunteering and Participating (NSGVP) provides some useful insights into Canadians' voluntary activities.

According to the NSGVP, over a quarter of all Canadians aged fifteen and older had engaged in unpaid activities as part of a group or organization during the preceding twelve months, a decline of 4 points compared with 1997 (Hall, McKeown, and Roberts 2001). The decline in the rate of volunteering between 1997 and 2000 meant that there were almost one million fewer volunteers in 2000, even though the population had grown by almost 2.5 percent. But those who were volunteering were giving more of their time. Between 1997 and 2000, the average number of hours volunteered increased from 149 hours to 162 hours. However, that increase was not enough to prevent the total number of volunteer hours dropping by about 5 percent between 1997 and 2000. This drop was equivalent to the loss of 29,000 full-time year-round volunteers (p. 32). Moreover, the top 25 percent of volunteers (or 7 percent of all Canadians aged fifteen and over) accounted for almost three-quarters of the total volunteer hours. The volunteer rate in 2000 was the same as in 1987, but those who were volunteering were volunteering significantly fewer hours than their counterparts in 1987 (191 hours).

The decline in volunteering between 1997 and 2000 stands in contrast with the growth that had occurred between 1987 and 1997. One of the causes of that growth was the tight labour market for young people (Hall, McKeown, and Roberts 2001, 12). Many young people saw volunteering as a way of gaining work-related experience when jobs were scarce. As employment opportunities for young people improved between 1997 and 2000, there was a significant decline in volunteering among Canadians aged twenty to twenty-four. However, the rate of volunteering fell in every other age group as well. Another possible cause of the growth in volunteering between 1987 and 1997 were the cuts in government programs and services that accompanied the drive to reduce the budget deficit. This may have encouraged more parents with children at home to volunteer in order to compensate for the cuts in government-provided social, educational, and recreational services (Reed and Selbee 2000).

When people were asked why they did not volunteer, the most common response (38 percent) was that they were donating money instead of time. Similarly, when those who did volunteer were asked why they did not volunteer more hours, almost a quarter of the volunteers responded that they were donating money instead. Giving money instead of time is becoming more prevalent: both figures were 5 percentage points higher than in 1997.

Not all volunteering is voluntary: over 7 percent of those who volunteered in 2000 were required to do so, some by their school, others by their employer or by the courts. This figure rose to 18 percent among those aged fifteen to twenty-four. Mandatory community service of one form or another added more than seventy-two million hours to the total in 2000.

Most volunteers (59 percent) limit their activities to a single organization, but significant numbers volunteer for two (26 percent) or more (15 percent) organizations. Cultural, arts, and recreational organizations head the list (23 percent), followed by social service organizations (20 percent), religious organizations (14 percent), educational and research organizations (13 percent), and health organizations (13 percent). The pattern was very similar in 1997.

Many Canadians also engage in informal volunteering, helping people on a one-to-one basis, as opposed to working through a charitable or nonprofit organization. According to the NSGVP, over three-quarters of Canadians gave their time to help people outside their household by driving them to appointments, doing the shopping, babysitting, or assisting with chores like house cleaning, yard work, and home maintenance. This was up 4 points from 1997. The percentage of Canadians who had helped people other than their relatives increased even more over the three-year period (from 71 percent to 79 percent), though there was a small drop in the percentage of people who had provided assistance to relatives who were not living with them (from 66 percent to 63 percent). More people were helping others with their housework, but fewer of them were assisting with tasks like writing letters or filling out forms.

Volunteering within the context of an organization or a group provides people with an opportunity to acquire practical skills. According to the NSGVP, typical volunteer activities include organizing or supervising events (57 percent), serving as a member of a board or a committee (41 percent), fundraising or canvassing (40 percent), and doing office work (30 percent). People appeared to be well aware that participating in those volunteer activities is an opportunity to improve various skills (see Figure 6.5). These ranged from interpersonal skills and communication skills to managerial skills and fundraising skills. Some of these skills, like public speaking and conducting meetings, are certainly likely to facilitate active involvement in politics. Volun-

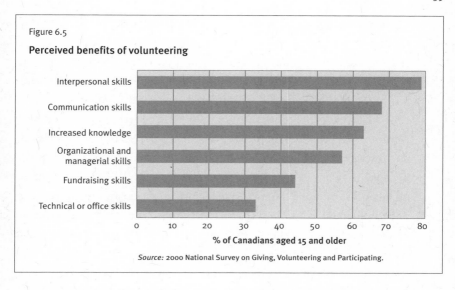

Figure 6.5

Perceived benefits of volunteering

% of Canadians aged 15 and older

Source: 2000 National Survey on Giving, Volunteering and Participating.

teering can also help people to become better informed about public affairs. Some of the people interviewed for the NSGVP reported that volunteering had enabled them to learn more about subjects ranging from health, the environment, and criminal justice to women's issues and political issues.

Who Volunteers?

Do these skill-building opportunities benefit those Canadians who need them most or do they benefit mainly those who have some skill base to begin with? We cannot answer this question directly, but we can see what sorts of people are most likely to volunteer. The answer is simple: the more education people have and the higher their household incomes, the more likely they are to volunteer. According to the NSGVP, university graduates were twice as likely (39 percent) to volunteer as people who left school without a high school diploma (19 percent), though they volunteered only a few more hours (166 hours) on average than the latter (154 hours). The decline in the rate of volunteering (down from 48 percent in 1997) was especially steep among university graduates. This parallels a decline in civic participation in the same group.

The rate of volunteering also declined substantially among people who were employed part-time (down from 44 percent to 33 percent), but part-time workers still volunteered in greater numbers than full-time workers (27 percent), the unemployed (25 percent), or people who were not part of the labour force at all (24 percent). Putnam (2000) suggests that people who are employed are more likely to volunteer because they are exposed to a more diverse array of social networks. As he notes, though, "There is a trade-off between time spent working and time spent volunteering, so the highest rate of volunteering is among part-time workers" (p. 119). However, the unemployed (175 hours) and those outside the labour force (193 hours) volunteered the greatest number of hours on average. Volunteering, it seems, is viewed as a way of enhancing employment prospects. Fully three-fifths of unemployed volunteers subscribed to the view that their volunteer activities would help them to get a job. This belief was even more prevalent (78 percent) among Canadians aged fifteen to twenty-four who were looking for work, though they volunteered relatively few hours (132 hours) on average.

Volunteering increases steadily with household income: two-fifths of Canadians with household incomes of $100,000 or more volunteered in 2000, compared with only a sixth of those with household incomes of less than $20,000. The poorest Canadians were the most generous with their time, volunteering an average of 207 hours, compared with 150 hours for the most affluent. Moreover, the largest increase in the average number of hours volunteered (up 59 hours) occurred among the least affluent volunteers.

The lowest rates of volunteering were found among Canadians aged twenty-four to thirty-four (24 percent) and among those aged sixty-five and over (18 percent). The demands of caring for young children may well be a factor for the former, while deteriorating health and diminished mobility probably limit volunteering among the latter. That said, those older Canadians who did volunteer were volunteering many more hours on average (269 hours) than younger Canadians and many more hours than in 1997 (202 hours). Similarly, widowed Canadians volunteered at a much lower rate than Canadians who were married, never married, separated, or divorced, but when they volunteered, they gave many more hours on average (253 hours) than other Canadians and many more than in 1997 (186 hours).

Volunteering was down among women and men alike in 2000, but women continued to volunteer at a slightly higher rate (28 percent) than men (25 percent), though male volunteers still volunteered more hours on average (170 hours) than their female counterparts (155 hours).

The only province to buck the trend of a declining rate of volunteer activities between 1997 and 2000 was Prince Edward Island. The steepest declines occurred in Ontario (from 32 percent to 25 percent) and British Columbia (from 32 percent to 26 percent). Along with Quebec (19 percent), these were also the two provinces with the lowest rates of volunteering in both 1997 and 2000. Residents of Saskatchewan remained the most likely (42 percent) to participate in volunteer activities, followed by Albertans (39 percent), Prince Edward Islanders (37 percent), Manitobans (36 percent), and Nova Scotians (34 percent). When it came to the number of hours volunteered, volunteers in Atlantic Canada were clearly more active than other Canadians, with the average ranging from 183 hours in Prince Edward Island to 206 hours in Newfoundland and Labrador. These four provinces also witnessed the largest increases in volunteer hours between 1997 and 2000. This might seem attributable to the high unemployment levels and poverty that characterize the region, but regardless of employment status and household income, Atlantic Canadians tend to participate in more volunteer activity than Canadians at large.

These provincial variations could well be cultural in origin. Certainly, the association between religion and volunteering points to the importance of norms and values. Canadians who attend religious services on a weekly basis were more likely (41 percent) to volunteer than those who do not (24 percent); they also volunteered more of their time (202 hours versus 149 hours). Even among regular worshippers, though, volunteering declined 5 points between 1997 and 2000. A similar pattern held for people who considered themselves to be very religious: they were more likely to volunteer and they volunteered more hours, but fewer of them volunteered than in 1997. It is worth noting that their activities were not limited to religious organizations. Simply having a religious affiliation, on the other hand, had only a modest effect on the rate of volunteering and on the number of hours volunteered.

How Generous Are Canadians?

Philanthropy may not be part of the definition of social capital, but Putnam (2000, 117) views it as an important indicator nonetheless, because philanthropy, like volunteering, is strongly predicted by civic engagement. According to the NSGVP, nine in ten Canadians aged fifteen and older had made financial or in-kind donations to charitable and nonprofit organizations in the twelve months leading up to the survey (Hall, McKeown, and Roberts 2001). The most frequent form of giving was a direct financial donation, followed by donations of clothing or household goods and donations of food (see Figure 6.6). Some of the giving appeared to be quite spontaneous: shoppers saw a collection box at the store checkout and were moved to deposit some cash. These spontaneous cash donations totalled just over $100 million. Canadians also provided indirect financial support to charitable and nonprofit organizations by purchasing items like chocolate bars, cookies, and poppies (70 percent), buying charity-sponsored raffle or lottery tickets (43 percent), and taking part in charity-sponsored gaming such as bingos or casinos (7 percent).

While the percentage of Canadians who donated money to charitable and nonprofit organizations remained stable between 1997 and 2000, the total number of charitable dollars given increased by 11 percent to more than $5 billion. This increase resulted only partly from population growth; mostly, people were donating more money. Between 1997 and 2000, the average annual donation increased by 8 percent to $259. One reason may be that this was a period of steady

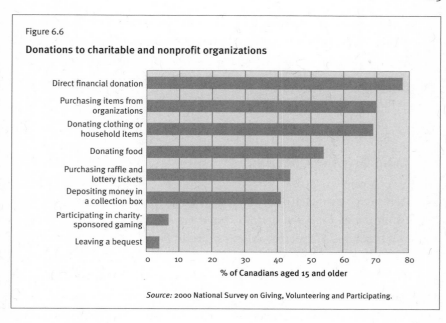

Figure 6.6

Donations to charitable and nonprofit organizations

% of Canadians aged 15 and older

Source: 2000 National Survey on Giving, Volunteering and Participating.

economic growth, rising employment, and higher incomes (Hall, McKeown, and Roberts 2001, 12). Another factor may be the introduction in the 1990s of enhanced tax incentives for charitable giving. However, over 80 percent of the total donations in 2000 were accounted for by just 25 percent of the donors. In 1997, too, the bulk of the charitable dollars came from a similarly small percentage of the total population aged fifteen and over. The median annual donation was only $73 in 2000, down from $76 in 1997.

According to the NSGVP, almost half of the money donated went to religious organizations. Another 20 percent went to health organizations and 10 percent to social service organizations. Almost one-third of Canadians had made a donation to a religious organization in the previous twelve months. The average annual contribution was much larger for religious organizations ($310) than for nonreligious organizations ($140). Most people who make charitable donations give money to more than one type of organization. In 2000, 31 percent contributed to two different types of organization, 22 percent to three different types, and 18 percent to four or more.

Giving is not confined to charitable donations. For example, the NSGVP reports that two-fifths of Canadians aged fifteen and over had given money directly to people outside their household. The money went to relatives (28 percent), the homeless and street people (19 percent), and other individuals (8 percent).

Who Gives to Charity?

How much people give to charity depends on their personal financial situation and not just on their generosity. The higher people's household income, the more likely they are to make a charitable donation and the larger the amount they are likely to give. According to the NSGVP, for example, 86 percent of Canadians with a gross household income of $100,000 or more were donors, compared with 63 percent of those with household incomes of less than $20,000. Given the disparity in their financial circumstances, though, we might reasonably have expected a larger difference in the average size of their donations. Donors with household incomes of less than $20,000 still managed to give an average of $142, up from $134 in 1997. Meanwhile, donors with household incomes of $100,000 or more gave an average of only $529, which was noticeably lower than their 1997 average of $608. Relative to their means, then, low-income Canadians appear to be considerably more generous than their affluent counterparts (Hall, McKeown, and Roberts 2001, 19).

Charitable giving also fell among university-educated Canadians. Eighty-four percent of university graduates made a charitable donation in 2000, down from 90 percent in 1997. And their average donation increased by only $7 to $480 in 2000. Education made surprisingly little difference to whether people donated money. Even among those with only a high school diploma, 80 percent were donors in 2000, up from 76 percent in 1997. Their average donation was $210. However, only 68 percent of Canadians with less than a high school education managed to make a donation.

People who were employed full-time were more likely (82 percent) to make a donation to a charitable or nonprofit organization than people who were working part-time (76 percent), unemployed (65 percent), or not part of the paid work force (73 percent). This may well reflect their financial circumstances.

There is also a clear relationship between age and charitable giving. Sixty-four percent of Canadians aged fifteen to twenty-four made a financial donation. This figure rose to 86 percent among Canadians aged thirty-five to forty-four, and then gradually fell off to 77 percent among those aged sixty-five and older. Charitable giving increased appreciably between 1997 and 2000 in the youngest age group. The percentage of donors rose by 5 points and the average size of donations went from $79 to $118. Average annual donations also increased substantially among those aged twenty-five to thirty-four, up from $159 in 1997 to $229 in 2000. Meanwhile, those aged sixty-five and older gave less in 2000 ($308) than they did in 1997 ($328) and fewer of them were donors (down 3 percentage points).

Whether people give, and how much they give, is influenced by their fundamental values (Hall, McKeown, and Roberts 2001). In this regard, it is interesting to note that women (81 percent) were more likely to be donors than men (75 percent), even though women tend to have lower incomes on average. Canadians who were married or living common-law were more likely to make a charitable donation (84 percent) than those who were single (66 percent), separated or divorced (72 percent), or widowed (77 percent), but widowed Canadians typically donated the most money ($328).

One value that is clearly related to charitable giving is religiosity. We have already seen that almost one-third of Canadians donated money to a religious organization in 2000. However, the influence of religion and religiosity was not confined to giving to religious organizations. People who considered themselves to be religious were also more likely to make donations (and to make larger donations) to nonreligious organizations. In 2000, the 11 percent of Canadians who characterized themselves as being very religious accounted for 29 percent of the total amount donated to charity. Similarly, there was a relationship between charitable giving and religious affiliation of any sort: 83 percent of Canadians claiming a religious affiliation made a charitable donation in 2000, compared with 72 percent of those claiming none, and their average annual contributions were twice as large ($296 as opposed to $146). The pattern was even stronger for those who attend services weekly: nine out of ten donated an average of $577 each, and their generosity extended beyond the religious sphere.

Nova Scotians (87 percent), Prince Edward Islanders (86 percent), and Newfoundlanders and Albertans (85 percent) were the most likely to make charitable donations in 2000, whereas Quebeckers and British Columbians (74 percent) were rather less likely to be donors. The donor rate in Alberta represented a very substantial increase over the 1997 figure (75 percent). Manitobans ($383) and Albertans ($369) gave the most, on average. It is not easy to account for the provincial variations. Undoubtedly a mix of factors is at work, including the state of the provincial economy, the sociodemographic makeup of the province, and the prevailing cultural norms and values, as well as the actions of the provincial government (Hall, McKeown, and Roberts 2001, 12, 19-20). Moreover, the fluctuations across time within individual provinces in both donor rates and the average amounts donated caution against drawing any general conclusions about the patterns observed at particular points in time.

Discussion

As Putnam's (2000) social capital thesis predicts, people who are active in voluntary associations are more politically engaged and more trusting. Whether this is because of their associational ties, we cannot say. If the social capital thesis is correct, though, the relatively high level of associational involvement in Canada, compared to that found in other established Western democracies, is a positive indicator of Canada's democratic health.

At the same time, an important fact must not be overlooked: the social biases that characterize political participation also characterize involvement in associational activities. E.E. Schattschneider (1960, 35) made the point some forty years ago: "The flaw in the pluralist heaven is that the heavenly chorus sings with a strong upper-class accent." Younger, less affluent, less educated Canadians are less likely to participate in politics *or* in networks of community engagement. There is little to suggest that community involvement is serving as a substitute for political engagement, and still less that it is offering an alternative way for the politically disengaged to make their needs and interests known.

To the extent that volunteering and charitable giving are indicators of social capital, poorer, less educated Canadians clearly have smaller stocks of social capital on which to trade. The same is true of members of visible minorities. Surprisingly, Quebeckers are also much less active in voluntary associations, and they are less likely to volunteer their time or to give to charitable causes. This does not square at all with the conventional image of the importance of the collectivity and collectivist values in Quebec. Why this should be so is something of a puzzle, but it could be a legacy of Quebec's Catholic past. According to the 1990 World Values Surveys, the median level of active membership in Catholic countries was a very substantial 10 points lower than the median for the other established Western democracies. The tradition of *étatisme* and state provision in Quebec may also have reduced the perceived importance of the voluntary sector.

Just as Putnam (2000) predicts, charitable giving, volunteering, and civic participation tend to go together (Hall, McKeown, and Roberts 2001). Citizens who engage in any one of these activities are more likely to participate in the others as well. For example, people who make charitable donations are also more likely to volunteer their time, to belong to civic associations, and to lend a helping hand to other people in their community.

We should not overstate Canadians' altruism; it exhibits some depth but its breadth is less impressive. According to the NSGVP, almost half of the total dollar value of all donations and two-fifths of all volunteer hours are provided by less than one-tenth of all Canadians. As Hall and his colleagues (Hall, McKeown, and Roberts 2001, 54) conclude, "What emerges is a portrait of a society in which most citizens provide modest, albeit important, levels of support to one another, but which also depends heavily upon the contributions of a small core of particularly engaged citizens."

CHAPTER 6

- Involvement in voluntary associations and political engagement go hand in hand. People who are active in voluntary associations pay more attention to politics, know more about politics, and participate more in politics than their social background characteristics would lead us to expect.

- Volunteering helps to build skills that are required for active participation in politics.

- In comparison with other established Western democracies, Canada has a relatively high level of active involvement in voluntary associations. Three out of every four Canadians have been active in one or more voluntary associations over the past five years.

- One out of every four Canadians volunteers as part of a group or organization.

- As many Canadians are volunteering as in 1987, but they are volunteering fewer hours. The top 25 percent of volunteers account for almost three-quarters of the total volunteer hours.

- Three out of every four Canadians volunteer on an informal basis.

- Less affluent, less educated Canadians are less likely to be active in voluntary associations, to volunteer their time, or to make charitable donations.

- Altruistic behaviours, like volunteering and making charitable donations, are more common among those who are actively involved in associational life, and vice versa.

7 ENGAGING CANADIANS

The notion of a democratic "audit" invites analogies with accounting, but the state of democratic citizenship is too complex to be reduced to a simple ledger, or a neat column of pluses and minuses. The evidence must be weighed to produce a picture of the strengths and weaknesses of democratic citizenship in Canada. This chapter draws the strands of the evidence together and highlights areas of strength and weakness. That assessment in turn suggests ways of enhancing democratic citizenship in Canada.

Significantly, the strengths are to be found not in the traditional arenas of democratic politics, but in areas that have more recently been identified as vital to a well-functioning democracy. One clear strength is the relatively high level of activity in voluntary associations in Canada. People who are involved in voluntary associations are typically better informed about politics, discuss politics more often, and participate in politics at a higher rate. They also tend to be more altruistic; they are more likely than others to volunteer and to donate their time and money, activities that undoubtedly contribute to the health and vitality of their communities.

Compared with citizens of most other established Western democracies, Canadians also show a greater readiness to make their opinions known and felt through various forms of protest activity. By traditional standards, such unconventional forms of political action as signing petitions and joining boycotts might have been diagnosed as signifying a withdrawal from democratic politics. But these same behaviours can also be interpreted as signs of democratic health. Having the right to speak out does not guarantee that citizens *will* speak out. So the fact that many Canadians do exercise their "voice" through lawful protest rather than remaining silent speaks to the health of democratic citizenship in Canada.

When more traditional forms of political participation come under scrutiny, however, the sources of concern emerge. Since 1988 voter turnout in federal elections has declined substantially. This decline is all the more worrying because much of it can be attributed to generational replacement. If young Canadians continue to vote at a lower rate than their predecessors, turnout could well continue to fall. This phenomenon is evident in elections in several other established Western democracies. But that is no cause for comfort, not least because levels of turnout in Canadian elections were low by international standards even before the recent decline began.

Declining voter turnout is not the only sign of disengagement from traditional electoral politics. There is reason to be just as concerned about how little Canadians know about the political world they occupy. Acquiring knowledge about politics is probably easier now than ever before, but it does require a minimal level of psychological and cognitive engagement. If political information is the "currency of citizenship" (Delli Carpini and Keeter 1996, 8), many Canadians are nearly broke. Even in the immediate aftermath of an election campaign in which the media bombarded Canadians with quantities of political information, significant numbers of Canadians were unable to name the party leaders. A majority of Canadians could not associate election promises with the correct parties, and only a minority could correctly identify which party was on the left and which was on the right. At issue, of course, is the critical question of how citizens can make informed choices when they lack even the most basic pieces of political information. Information shortcuts can help, but they are no panacea.

Another sign of disengagement is the small and diminishing number of Canadians who take an active part in election campaigns. Relatively few Canadians have ever belonged to a political party, and there is a good deal of skepticism about the idea that joining a political party is the best way to achieve change. That said, even fewer Canadians have ever belonged to an interest group, and the level of party membership in Canada does not appear to be unusually low by comparison with other established democracies.

It is tempting to suppose that Canadians are turning to unconventional forms of political participation because they see political parties as ineffective and unresponsive. If the conventional avenues of political participation are not working, why not find more meaningful forms of political participation? But, for most people at least, the evidence does not support that line of speculation. In fact, one of the most striking findings to emerge from this audit is the extent to which different forms of political engagement tend go together. Canadians who are active in their communities, sign petitions, and take part in boycotts are often the same Canadians who are the most likely to vote, to work on a political campaign, and to join a political party or an interest group. This core of Canadians follows politics closely, knows what is going on, and takes an active part in public life.

However, many Canadians do none of these things. They pay scant attention to the news, they know little or nothing about what is happening politically, and they do not even bother to vote. That finding might not be worrisome if the disengaged were a small group of people sprinkled randomly throughout the population. The problem is that this group is not small and the disengaged Canadians are not drawn equally from every walk of life. On the contrary, in Canada as elsewhere, there is a strong association between structural inequalities in society and lack of engagement with democratic politics.

Identifying the Democratic Divides

The most dramatic democratic divide is generational. Young Canadians are less interested in politics, they pay less attention to news about politics in the media, and they know less about what is going on, even on matters like globalization. They are less likely than older Canadians to vote or to have belonged to a political party. Indeed, much of the decline in turnout in federal elections since 1988 can be explained by generational replacement. And there is no evidence that these young people are turning to other, more meaningful ways of making their voices heard. Young Canadians are even less likely than older Canadians to have belonged to an interest group working for change, and they are the least likely to have engaged in any form of protest behaviour or to have been active in a voluntary association.

Grassroots activism is not taking the place of traditional modes of engagement. On the contrary, the young people who are active at the grassroots level are often the same young Canadians who turn out to vote or who belong to a political party. What distinguishes this core of highly engaged young people from their contemporaries is their level of education: they are much more likely to have finished university. Young university graduates show little indication of increasing disengagement. What is alarming is the level of disengagement among those young people who lack even a high school education.

Age is not the only democratic divide. Material circumstances and education are also critical. Canadians who struggle at the economic margins of society typically have less interest in politics. As a result, they are often poorly acquainted with such basic political facts as the names of the party leaders or where the parties stand. They also participate in politics at much lower rates, whether voting, belonging to a political party, or joining an interest group. In stark contrast to the predemocratic days when protest was the only voice of the poor, political protest is today much more common among the affluent. The same holds for involvement in voluntary associations, though in some types of groups — notably women's groups — low-income Canadians are somewhat more active than their affluent counterparts.

The poor do not lack civic spirit. Indeed, relative to their means, poor Canadians could be considered more charitable than wealthy Canadians. Moreover, differences in educational attainment only partly explain the democratic divide between the haves and the have-nots in Canadian society. The hard truth is that living at the margins is demanding, and it takes time and energy to follow politics closely and to participate in politics. It also requires money. Political engagement is not free. The costs of subscribing to a newspaper, hiring a babysitter, or travelling to a meeting may seem inconsequential to the affluent, but for the poor, these costs amount to real impediments to active engagement. Then there is the matter of the perceived stakes: poorer Canadians may simply feel that they are not really listened to and that there is little to be gained from active engagement, especially in traditional partisan politics.

Similar differences in the perceived stakes may help to explain the gender gaps in political engagement. Women are typically less interested in politics than men are, pay less attention to what is going on politically, and discuss politics less. Women also typically have smaller stocks of political information. These gender gaps cannot be explained by the fact that the average Canadian woman has less education and a lower income than her male counterpart. Nor is it explained by the "double day" of employment and family responsibilities confronted by many women. What is truly striking is that affluent women are no better informed than men with only average household incomes. And women with some postsecondary education are no better informed than men without a high school diploma.

Similar gender gaps are evident in other established Western democracies, and it is difficult to pinpoint their exact cause. Possible causes include the lack of women in elected office and the norms of behaviour that govern the conduct of politics. The media reinforce these norms by framing politics as an unending battle for supremacy. Yet another possibility is the perceived remoteness of politics in Ottawa from many women's day-to-day concerns. It is telling that when people are asked about their knowledge of school board elections, the gender gap reverses: women know more than men.

Despite the gender gaps in interest and information, women are just as likely as men to have been members of an interest group and only slightly less likely than men to have belonged to a political party at some point in their lives. There is also little sign of a gender gap for involvement in protest politics or active membership in voluntary associations. And women turn out to vote at the same rate as men.

One reason women participate in traditional forms of politics at the same levels as men relates to a stronger sense of duty. Women are more likely than men to say that they would feel guilty if they did not vote. What remains to be seen is whether this sense of moral obligation will continue to counterbalance lack of interest. The gender gap in political interest is widest among young Canadians: young women are typically even less interested in politics than are young men. At the same time, young Canadians are less likely to feel that they ought to vote.

Given the dearth of visible minorities in elected office and the racial biases that remain in Canadian society, one might expect race to form another democratic divide. But there is little evidence of a racial divide. The data show that members of visible minorities are as interested (or not) in politics as other Canadians. Their patterns of media usage are also very similar, and they are actually more likely to go on-line in search of information about politics. Rates of party membership are similar, too. Indeed, members of visible minorities were more likely than others to have helped out in the 2000 election campaign. Still, members of visible minorities are less likely to talk about politics with other people, and they are somewhat less informed than other Canadians. They are also less likely to vote, though much of the turnout gap has to do with the fact that members of visible minorities tend to be younger on average, and younger people are less likely to vote. Members of visible minorities are also less likely to have belonged to an interest group, to have engaged in acts of political protest, or to have been active in a voluntary association. However, they are as active as other Canadians in women's and environmental groups and more active in religious and ethnic organizations.

The picture of democratic engagement among Canadians born outside the country is similarly mixed. Foreign-born Canadians tend to be more interested in politics than the Canadian born, but they are less likely to have belonged to a political party or to have taken part in protest activities. But then, they may have had less opportunity to do so. When people arrived in Canada is typically more important than whether they are immigrants or not. Recent arrivals are less likely to rely on the newspaper for information about politics, but they are more likely to turn to the Internet, perhaps because they want to keep abreast of politics in their country of origin. The Internet is global, and newspapers are more local. Recent arrivals are less likely to be informed about Canadian politics, they are less likely to vote, and they are less likely to be actively involved in voluntary associations. This is understandable. Immigrants have had less time to acclimatize themselves to the political practices and norms of their new country, and less time to accumulate knowledge of Canada's politics. Moreover, the challenge of adjusting to a new environment may leave them less time and energy to spend on politics. Once established, immigrants typically display levels of political engagement similar to their Canadian-born counterparts. This conclusion mirrors that of earlier studies conducted by Jerome Black (1982; 1987) and by Tina Chui and her colleagues (Chui, Curtis, and Lambert 1991).

What matters more is where people live. Quebeckers are typically less engaged than other Canadians. That conclusion holds regardless of whether we consider political interest, using the Internet to get political information, or talking about politics with other people. It also holds for civic engagement more generally. Quebeckers are less active in voluntary associations and they are less likely to volunteer or to make charitable donations. The one form of engagement that is more common in Quebec than elsewhere is membership in a political party, which may reflect the importance of a dues-paying mass membership to the Parti Québécois.

Residents of Saskatchewan are also more likely than other Canadians to have belonged to a political party. Intriguingly, this holds despite the fact that, like Quebeckers, they, too, are less interested in politics, less likely to go on-line for political information, and less likely to make politics a topic of conversation. But unlike Quebeckers, residents of Saskatchewan rank high when it comes to associational involvement and volunteering, findings that reflect, perhaps, the residuals of Saskatchewan's collectivist tradition. Even so, Saskatch-ewan has witnessed one of the largest declines in both federal and provincial voter turnout over the past decade.

With one notable exception, the most engaged citizens are to be found in Alberta. Albertans rank high on political interest, political discussion, using the Internet as a source of political information, and party membership. They also volunteer and give more than other Canadians. Yet they are the least likely to turn out to vote in provin-cial elections and among the least likely to vote in federal elections. The low turnout in provincial elections could reflect the long history of one-party dominance in the province, while the low turnout in fed-eral elections may have its roots in regional alienation. Whatever the reasons, the disjuncture between turnout to vote and other forms of political and civic engagement in the province is striking. Ontario presents a similar picture: low turnout in both provincial and federal elections, combined with higher-than-average levels of political inter-est, Internet use, reliance on newspapers for information, and cam-paign activity. Unlike Albertans, however, Ontarians rank quite low on party membership and volunteering. Manitobans share Ontarians' interest in politics and heavier reliance on the press for news, but they vote in higher numbers than Ontarians, at least in provincial elections, and they rank high on measures of associational involve-ment and volunteering.

Atlantic Canadians are typically close to the Canadian average on most indicators of engagement, though the lowest (Newfoundland and Labrador) and highest (Prince Edward Island) average turnouts in recent federal elections are both to be found in the region. Nova Sco-tians rank high when it comes to involvement in the larger commu-nity: they are more active in voluntary associations than average, and they volunteer and give in greater numbers. Aside from this, there are no notable patterns in the region.

The fact that Atlantic Canadians do not rank below the Canadian average on most dimensions of political and civic engagement sug-gests that regional disparities in income and education cannot explain the differences observed across the country. Rather, the patterns seem to owe more to variations in the nature of politics and the political cultures of the different provinces.

Certainly, the patterns cannot be explained by differences in urbanization. Contrary to conventional wisdom, rural Canadians are typically no more engaged than their urban counterparts. In fact, they turn out to be less likely than city-dwellers to rely on newspapers for information about politics. The single exception relates to party membership: rural Canadians are more likely to have belonged to a political party. In general, though, little distinguishes rural and urban Canadians when it comes to political engagement.

It is difficult to reach a conclusion about the impact of the size of a political unit. Turnout is higher in provincial elections than it is in federal elections in every province except Ontario, Alberta, and Manitoba. Similarly, turnout is higher in territorial elections than it is in federal elections. On the other hand, turnout to vote in some of Canada's largest cities is lower than it is in both federal and provincial elections in the same province. In their study of municipal elections in Ontario, Kushner and his colleagues (Kushner, Siegel, and Stanwick 1997) found an association between size and turnout: turnout was lowest in large municipalities and highest in the smallest municipalities. But even in the small municipalities, turnout was typically lower than the average turnout in federal or provincial elections in the province. Nor is there any apparent association between the size of a province and the turnout to vote in either federal or provincial elections. Since 1990, for example, average turnout in federal and provincial elections has been very similar in New Brunswick and Quebec, despite the disparities in their size. The same is true of Saskatchewan and British Columbia.

Comparing orientations toward politics at the three levels of government is difficult, primarily because of the lack of available survey evidence. The limited data that are available suggest strikingly similar patterns when it comes to knowledge of politics at the three levels: large numbers of people can name the chief executive (be it the prime minister, premier, or mayor), but knowledge levels drop off sharply when people are asked to name other political actors.

Enhancing Democratic Citizenship

The challenges that emerge from this audit of democratic citizenship are clear. One is to find ways of re-engaging young citizens. A second is how to create a more informed citizenry, and a third concerns how to narrow the existing democratic divides. Identifying the challenges is easier than setting out solutions to such complex problems. But it is possible to scan the horizons to see solutions others have turned to, and with what effect.

RE-ENGAGING YOUNG CANADIANS

Turnout in federal elections has declined massively among young Canadians since 1988. A recent study in the United States is suggestive; it points to the importance of getting young citizens to vote for the first time. Once young people have paid the "start-up costs of voting," they are likely to keep on voting (Plutzer 2002). So, what can be done to reduce the start-up costs for young Canadians? First, political parties have a role to play. Political parties are representative institutions, and if they make little effort to mobilize the citizenry, then citizens are less likely to vote. Regardless of which party they heard from, people who reported being contacted by a political party or a candidate during the 2000 campaign were more likely to vote. As the data in Chapter 5 demonstrated, young Canadians were much less likely than others to report being contacted. The clear implication is that a concerted get-out-the-vote effort by the political parties could well help to reverse the downward trend in voting among the young.

Second, the problems with the permanent voters list need to be resolved (see Courtney 2004). In 2000 young Canadians were the segment of the population least likely to have received a voter information card, and the most likely to have found it difficult to get their names on the permanent voters list. Part of the problem is that young people are much more mobile; they are likely to be tenants rather than homeowners. They are also less likely to file tax returns (which is one way that the list is updated). So they are either not on the list or listed under the wrong address. If these flaws in the system can be addressed, young people will find it easier to vote.

In addition to these short-term solutions, various long-term solutions should be considered. Early experiences can lay the foundation for a lifetime of democratic engagement. In this regard, research on volunteering may hold broader lessons for civic engagement. Michael Hall and his colleagues (Hall, McKeown, and Roberts 2001, 39) found that there was a clear, albeit weakening, connection between volunteering and people's experiences early in life. Volunteering rates were higher, for example, among people who had been active in student government, who had a parent who spent time volunteering, or who belonged to a youth group. Having been helped by others in early life was also a motivating factor. If volunteering in adulthood is encouraged by experiences during people's formative years, the trend toward mandatory community service in high school could have effects that persist into later life. And, as the evidence presented in Chapter 6 indicated, volunteering tends to go hand in hand with civic engagement.

In addition, a large US survey of students in grades nine to twelve and their parents indicates that community service enhances students' knowledge of politics. It also encourages more discussion of politics with their parents, and fosters a sense of political competence (Niemi, Hepburn, and Chapman 2000). However, these benefits only seem to accrue if the amount of service is substantial. Moreover, the authors of this study sound an important cautionary note: students who were involved in few other activities, who had lower grades, and whose parents did not perform any community service were much less likely to be involved in community service themselves. In other words, unless community service is universal, it risks deepening the democratic divides. For this reason Benjamin Barber (1992) argues forcefully that service in the community should be made mandatory rather than voluntary. But as Hepburn and her colleagues (Hepburn, Niemi, and Chapman 2000, 621) ask, "If service is required, will the students forced to participate learn from it?"

Community service seems to be most beneficial when it takes the form of "service learning." This term denotes service that is actually incorporated into high school courses in ways that encourage both awareness of the related social and political issues and reflection upon the experience (Hepburn, Niemi, and Chapman 2000; Galston 2001). The rationale for service learning is found in John Dewey's (1916; 1938) argument that schooling must be linked to real-world experience. Some educators have raised concerns, though, about the possible partisan and ideological connotations of training for citizenship.

What about civic education classes? Many see civic courses as a way of enhancing democratic engagement, and the province of Ontario actually introduced a mandatory civics course for grade ten students in fall 2000 (Myers 2000). But some critical questions remain unanswered:

> When should students receive civics/government instruc-
> tion? ... What classroom and extra-classroom methods are
> best suited to teaching about government? How much train-
> ing should there be in research methods? Are the skills
> needed for citizenship the same as the skills needed for polit-
> ical analysis? What kind of instruction, if any, will make
> young people less cynical about (yet appropriately skeptical
> of) politicians (Niemi and Smith 2001, 286)?

For all the interest in revitalizing civic education, surprisingly little research systematically evaluates its benefits, especially over the long term (Niemi and Smith 2001). This is partly because conventional wisdom has long held that civic courses are ineffective. Most of the evidence about the effectiveness of civics education comes from the United States, where the experience has been mixed. The proportion of US high school students taking American government courses has risen steadily since 1980. According to a recent study (Niemi and Smith 2001), nearly 80 percent of graduating seniors have had a government class at some stage of their high school education. And yet knowledge of politics remains low and concern about political disengagement on the part of young adults has continued to grow. Indeed, the 1998 Civics Assessment, conducted as part of the National

Assessment of Educational Progress mandated by the US Congress, found that only a quarter of high school seniors met or exceeded the standard of proficiency, while over a third tested below basic, "indicating near-total civic ignorance" (Galston 2001, 221). Evidently, civic education can fail.

Others believe that civics education can be effective, but much depends on the content (Niemi and Junn 1998; Galston 2001). Ken Osborne (1988, 228), for example, suggests that what is needed is "a genuinely political education, if the schools are to produce informed, participating citizens," and that this means bringing real-world political issues into the classroom (see also Osborne 2000). In a similar vein, Richard Niemi and Jane Junn (1998, 150) have been critical of "the Pollyannaish view of politics" that is encouraged when civics education is devoid of any serious discussion of partisan politics and interest groups. "If students can be taught to understand that political parties and interest groups form to promote and protect legitimate differences in points of view," they argue, "they would be in a much better position to understand, appreciate, and participate in the political process." It is not just a matter of *what* is taught in civics classes, but *how* it is taught (Osborne 1988). Context matters, and a number of commentators have pointed to the importance of fostering a democratic classroom climate so that students are not just learning about democratic skills and dispositions but actually practising them (Levin 2000; Sears and Perry 2000). Timing also appears to be important: high school government courses seem to be most effective when they are taken in grade twelve rather than earlier in a student's career (Niemi and Junn 1998).

The intractable problem with solutions like mandatory service learning and required civics courses is that they cannot reach those who are no longer in school. Indeed, for the long term, the key to democratic engagement may simply be to keep more young people in school. As William Galston (2001, 219) observes, "all education is civic education in the sense that individuals' level of general educational attainment significantly affects their level of political knowledge as well as the quantity and character of their political participation." Indeed, the one group of young people that has been immune to the trend toward disengagement is university graduates. It is hardly surprising that university graduates are typically the most engaged citizens, because becoming a well-informed citizen requires considerable cognitive capacity. Consider one public opinion expert's advice:

> Whenever you read or see political material, exercise skepticism. Figure out motivations and ideologies in the newspaper, magazine, or television show you are looking at; watch for its editorial thrust and for slants in the news or information it presents. What stories are made prominent? Why? What is ignored? Who is quoted, and why? What evaluative material is slipped in? Try to read between the lines, spotting what the reporter did not say, and try to dig out obscure but important bits that contradict the main story line (Page 1996, 125-6).

These tasks will be quite beyond the capabilities of people who do not even possess basic literacy skills, which are precisely what many of Canada's high school dropouts lack (Applied Research Branch 2000). Canada's dropout rates appear to be more or less in line with other OECD (Organisation for Economic Co-operation and Development) countries, but Canadian dropouts typically have much lower levels of literacy. This is because "a large proportion of those who drop out do so at an early age and at low levels of education ... Almost one third drop out with Grade 9 education or less and almost two thirds drop out with Grade 10 or less ... The earlier that students drop out, the less knowledge and fewer skills that they will have accumulated" (Applied Research Branch 2000, 13-14). And, we could add, the less likely they are to have any interest in politics or to be acquainted with the sorts of political information required for meaningful engagement in democratic politics.

CREATING A MORE INFORMED CITIZENRY

There is a lively debate about whether citizens really need to know "textbook facts" about their political world to make adequately informed decisions about how to vote. Yet one of the clearest messages to emerge from this audit of democratic citizenship is that information matters. Indeed, information is the essential prerequisite of responsive and responsible government: governments cannot be held accountable if citizens do not know what those in power have been doing. Knowing who the key political actors are may not be that consequential in itself, but "differences in knowledge of several such 'minor' facts are diagnostic of more profound differences in the amount and accuracy of contextual information voters bring to their judgments" (Converse 2000, 333; see also Neuman 1986; Delli Carpini and Keeter 1996).

Having a store of contextual information is important because it helps people to make sense of and to impart meaning to new pieces of information. This is the so-called Matthew principle: "to them that hath shall be given," or as Converse (2000, 335) puts it more colloquially, "them what has, gets." This principle clearly applies to campaign learning. Election campaigns actually widen the knowledge gap: those who know the most about politics in general end up learning the most, while those who know little to begin with learn the least. And information shortcuts often end up helping those who need them least, because those who need these shortcuts the most often lack the contextual information required to take advantage of them.

More important, opinion on some significant policy issues would very likely be different if Canadians were better informed about politics. This is especially true when people are misinformed about policy-relevant facts. Informed opinion on social policy questions is typically more liberal than actual opinion. The same holds for opinions about some fiscal matters and some issues concerning the role of the state versus the market. Because information can affect policy preferences and political attitudes, people who share similar background characteristics may hold very different opinions, depending on how well informed they are. This finding implies that people who are poorly informed are more likely to get it "wrong" when it comes to translating their preferences into appropriate political choices.

The extent to which citizens are informed is not a function of their own abilities and motivation alone: "Voters are not fools ... The electorate behaves about as rationally and responsibly as we should expect, given the clarity of the alternatives presented to it and the character of the information available to it" (Key 1966, 7). The main sources of information for citizens are the media and political actors, neither of which necessarily have a vested interest in disseminating the objective facts. Politicians and other political actors may be tempted to deploy facts in self-serving ways to build support for their preferred positions. If politicians obfuscate and political parties fail to articulate clear alternatives, is there reason to be surprised if many citizens end up with only a vague or confused sense of what the politicians stand for?

However, even when politicians and political parties take clear stands, their messages do not necessarily reach the voters. Economic incentives encourage the media to put the emphasis on entertaining first and informing only second (Zaller 1999). Whether publicly or privately owned, broadcasters have to be concerned about audience share, just as the print media are preoccupied with circulation figures. Consequently, a party's issue positions may receive only token coverage if what the party is saying or doing is not deemed newsworthy, and newsworthiness is often determined by standings in the polls. When an issue position does receive extensive coverage, even poorly informed voters have the opportunity to learn about it.

A striking finding from recent election data is that even otherwise relatively well-informed voters had difficulty matching the parties with their promises, or classifying the parties in terms of left and right. Providing more coverage of the issues and being more even-handed in the amount of coverage provided to the various political parties would help to raise the mean level of knowledge about the parties and their stands.

Narrowing the Democratic Divides

When it comes to inclusiveness and responsiveness, diminishing the variance in political knowledge is at least as important as raising the mean. Proposals to increase the amount of information available to voters by regulating the nature and amount of coverage that broadcasters provide are going to benefit only those who are following politics to begin with. The same objection applies to another suggested solution, namely, having longer campaigns (Moore 1987). The idea is that longer election campaigns would give people more time to learn about the issues. In theory, election campaigns represent an unparalleled opportunity to engage voters (Cappella and Jamieson 1997, 241). Indeed, Popkin (1991) has likened elections to civics education, with political parties as the teachers. In practice, though, the least informed typically also learn the least during a campaign.

Eveland and Scheufele (2000, 216) actually go so far as to argue that increasing the amount of political information (and participation) "among some groups but not others ... could be worse for democracy than no overall increase at all." This is especially true "when the group increasing in knowledge or participation is already politically advantaged and has interests at odds with the disadvantaged group." At issue is not just the low level of knowledge per se, but the uneven *social* distribution of knowledge. Older Canadians know more than younger Canadians, affluent Canadians know more than poor Canadians, and men know more than women. The worry is that the needs and wants of affluent, older men are the most likely to be reflected in collective expressions of opinion. Differences would be larger on important questions of public policy if the young, the poor, and women were better informed. To the extent that this is so, public policy may well be less responsive to their needs and interests. Communications scholars put the point bluntly: "When there are disparities across social groups in political knowledge and participation, democracy is at least a little less democratic, regardless of the underlying reasons for these inequities" (Eveland and Scheufele 2000, 216).

The observation that information shortfalls are associated with democratic divides points to a deeper issue: why are some Canadians not better informed about politics? There is no shortage of potential answers to that question, and many of them take us back to the more basic question of why interest in politics is not higher. The pre-eminent point to acknowledge is that the costs of acquiring information are higher for some citizens than for others. The cost of subscribing to a daily newspaper, cable television, or an Internet access service may be beyond the reach of poor families. However, the effects of structural inequalities run deeper than differences in the costs of becoming informed. As Page and Shapiro (1992, 164) note, when it comes to the dissemination of political information, economic inequality tends to win out over political equality: "A large corporation has a much better chance of learning how a tax bill will affect it than do many unorganized taxpayers with small, diffuse interests."

The challenge, then, is to narrow the information gap by "lifting the bottom." Information presumes interest. If people have little or no interest in political affairs, they are unlikely to invest time and energy in seeking out political information. This is why John Zaller (1999, 2) argues that the problem is not lack of informational content in the media. On the contrary, he maintains, large numbers of citizens are being turned off by a style of politics and political communication that is "stilted, overly rationalistic, and just plain dull." Zaller takes intellectuals to task for bemoaning the rise of "infotainment" journalism when they should be seeing it as a way of re-engaging citizens' interest in politics. His point is that "infotainment" journalism offers citizens a way to fulfill "the informational obligations of citizenship ... with less effort and more pleasure" (p. 3). Zaller supports this seemingly heretical suggestion by pointing to the disappointing experience with the free television-time experiment in the 1996 US presidential election. The provision of large blocks of free television time on the three major networks was greeted with a singular lack of enthusiasm on the part of the candidates, the networks, and the electorate alike.

Rather than "fact-packed and informationally turgid" media content, Zaller argues, what is required are more stories that truly engage
people. Dan Quayle's attack on the television character Murphy Brown
is one case in point. The former US vice-president took the fictional
character to task for having a child outside marriage. By focusing so
much coverage on this seemingly trivial incident, the media succeeded in making "the family values debate accessible to Americans in
a way that traditional political rhetoric did not" (Zaller 1999, 16). The
2000 federal election provided a Canadian analogue to the Murphy
Brown story in the form of the Doris Day petition. The CBC comedy
program *This Hour Has 22 Minutes* satirized the Alliance party's
stand on direct democracy by inviting Canadians to add their names
to a petition requesting that the party's leader, Stockwell Day, be
required to change his name to Doris Day. Over one million people
signed the petition through the show's Web site. There was a serious
point: to demonstrate how easy it was to gather the requisite number
of signatures required to initiate a binding referendum. And that point
supports Zaller's contribution that some attention to politics is better
than no attention at all, especially when viewers are being informed as
well as entertained. A recent study by Matthew Baum (2002) also lends
some support to this argument. He found that "due to selective political
coverage by the entertainment-oriented soft news media, many otherwise politically inattentive individuals are exposed to information
about high-profile political issues, most prominently foreign policy
crises, as an incidental by-product of seeking entertainment" (p. 91).

Zaller also takes a sanguine view of "horserace journalism." This is
coverage that focuses on "who is ahead, who is behind, who is gaining,
who is losing, what campaign strategy is being followed, and what the
impact of campaign activities is on the candidate's chances of winning" (Joslyn 1984, 133). In Canada, as elsewhere, television news coverage seems preoccupied with the horse race in general and with the
leaders' abilities as campaigners in particular, to the neglect of serious coverage of the issues (Mendelsohn 1993; 1996; Mendelsohn and
Nadeau 1999). In Zaller's view, the unanimous condemning of the
prevalence of this type of coverage is wrong. Horserace coverage, he

argues, is not devoid of substantive content, but can provide citizens with "a palatable mix of entertainment, information, debate, and politically useful cues," especially about the opinions of relevant groups (Zaller 1999, 19). Above all, though, this style of coverage appeals to millions of voters by making politics a spectator sport. If making politics seem like a game gets people to pay attention, Zaller maintains, then this is all to the good.

But does the prevalence of the "game frame" get viewers to tune in, or does it simply turn them off? There is evidence, for example, that some people are less active politically because they want to avoid conflict (Mansbridge 1980; Ulbig and Funk 1999; Mutz 2002). If media coverage reinforces the perception that politics is all about confrontation and competition, it may discourage such people from being politically active. We also need to ask what sort of people typically "spend many leisure hours" (Zaller 1999, 18) watching sports events on television. The audience for the sporting events that typically dominate the airwaves is still predominantly male, and politics may be just another game watched by men. After all, the players are still mostly men. We know that women are less likely than men to follow politics closely. It is not clear whether this is related to the way politics is covered, but there is certainly cause to wonder. These are the sorts of questions, in our view, that need to be answered before Zaller's enthusiasm for horserace journalism can be readily embraced. But Zaller is surely right to encourage us to think outside the box when it comes to ways of stimulating greater political awareness.

Political interest is likely to be higher to the extent that citizens see a link between political affairs and their own lives. If politics is perceived to be remote and abstract, or worse yet, corrupt and self-serving, citizens will simply tune out. Globalization and market rhetoric encourage the view that governments are not only relatively powerless in the face of global economic forces, but govern best when they govern least. That view is certainly open to challenge, but it should come as little surprise to discover that many citizens seem to have internalized the message that politics just does not matter very much.

This message has perhaps been encouraged by changes in the way that the media cover politics. Over the past two decades, media coverage in Canada (as in the United States) has taken on an increasingly negative tone; straight reporting of the facts has become subordinate to interpretation and evaluation, and the framing of stories too often highlights partisan calculation, conflict, and personal motives. The result, Richard Nadeau and Thierry Giasson (2003, 9) suggest, is a "devalued concept of politics" that discredits the electoral process "by reducing the broad debates of society to simple partisan issues." They go on to advocate a shift to "public journalism," or "civic journalism," as an antidote. This is a type of political reporting that puts citizens and their needs at the forefront of coverage: "From this angle, electoral news must principally focus on citizens' questions about issues they consider to be priorities and on party positions concerning these precise issues. The reporting in public journalism must cover campaigns by uncovering ordinary citizens' experiences" (p. 18). The task of the journalist is to contextualize social issues and to foster debate with citizens about the proffered solutions. While admittedly somewhat idealistic, this approach has been practised in parts of the United States for the past dozen years; it has also been associated with significant gains in citizens' political knowledge. Changing media practices is no easy task, though, given the constraints under which journalists work, be they organizational, technical, financial, or the constraints of the genre itself (see Nadeau and Giasson 2003).

The single most important step that can be taken to narrow the democratic divides is to increase the number of Canadians who complete high school and go on to postsecondary education. One of the central findings to emerge from this audit of democratic citizenship is just how well education serves democracy. The more education people have, the more interested they are in politics, the more attention they pay to news about politics, and the more they know about politics. And the more education people have, the more likely they are to vote, to belong to a political party or an interest group, to sign petitions and join in boycotts, and to be active in their communities. Education does not just provide citizens with better tools for democratic citizenship, it also provides them with the inclination for it.

A recent report by the Applied Research Branch of Human Resources Development Canada (2000, 58) outlines some of the policy options for encouraging more Canadians to complete their high school education: "awareness campaigns, raising the legal age at which youth can leave school, improving literacy, modifying programs for those who have difficulties with academic programs, developing alternative pathways to the workplace, policies directed to families, schools and the community, lowering the minimum wage, and developing non-accreditation learning options."

The HRDC report makes the point that lowering the dropout rate is good economic sense. The report estimates that the total monetary rate of return to society for completing high school as opposed to stopping at grade ten is 17 percent. But a lower dropout rate is not only good for the Canadian economy; it is also good for Canadian democracy. More Canadians would be equipped with the cognitive skills and the motivation needed to be active and engaged citizens. Keeping students in school would also help to address the other root cause of democratic disengagement, namely poverty. The same study makes the relationship between socioeconomic factors and dropping out clear. Poor children are at greater risk of dropping out, and dropping out makes a lifetime of poverty more likely.

Citizenship Today

The picture of democratic citizenship in Canada is mixed. A core of highly engaged citizens pays close attention to politics and takes an active part in civic life. At the same time, a very significant minority of Canadians knows little about politics and cares less. Most disturbing, perhaps, is the evidence of deep pockets of political ignorance within certain groups in Canadian society. These democratic deficits diminish the inclusiveness and impair the responsiveness of Canadian democracy. And the most striking deficits are those defined by material circumstances, age, and gender. Of course there are poor young women who are highly engaged in civic life, just as there are affluent older men who are not. But the association between democratic engagement and social background is indisputable.

The systematic nature of this association should make us look to its deeper causes. The numerical underrepresentation of certain groups in Canada's political institutions is one factor. And patterns of media coverage and the conduct of election campaigns are implicated. But the roots of democratic disengagement also lie deep in the structural inequalities that characterize Canadian society. To the extent that they do, only by tackling those inequalities can democratic citizenship in Canada become truly inclusive.

Discussion Questions

Chapter 1: Auditing Democratic Citizenship

1 What attributes do you think are needed to be an effective citizen?
2 Do you think that the composition of democratic institutions ought to reflect the social makeup of the population?
3 What criteria should be used to judge whether the media are doing a good job of covering politics?
4 What functions do you think political parties should perform in an electoral democracy?
5 Which seems more responsive to citizens' needs and wants: the federal government, your provincial or territorial government, or your municipal government? Why?
6 How might elections affect the quality of democratic citizenship?

Chapter 2: How Much Attention Do Canadians Pay to Politics?

1 Why do you think women tend to be less interested in politics than men?
2 Why do you think so many young Canadians are paying little attention to politics?
3 Do you think that the concerns about dependence on television for information about politics are justified?
4 How could the Internet be used to enhance Canadians' interest in politics?
5 What factors encouraged your interest in politics?
6 Is there something about politics itself that causes so many citizens to "tune out"? If so, how might this be changed?

Chapter 3: What Do Canadians Know about Politics?

1 Why do you think levels of knowledge about politics are so low?
2 Why do you think Canadians know less about international affairs than citizens of many other established Western democracies?
3 What do people need to know about politics in order to be effective citizens?
4 What steps could be taken to encourage Canadians to learn more about political affairs?
5 Why do you think election campaigns are not doing more to inform Canadians?
6 Which do you know more about: federal politics, politics in your province or territory, or local politics? Why?

Chapter 4: Can Canadians Get By with Less Information?

1 In what sense is it rational (or not) for people to rely on information short-cuts?

2 Why do you think information is associated with more liberal opinions on questions of social policy, like the death penalty, abortion, and gender roles?

3 Why do you think levels of misinformation are so high?

4 Why do you think that people who pay attention to the media are often prone to getting policy-relevant facts wrong?

5 What steps could be taken to correct misinformation?

6 If you were working with an antipoverty group, how would you go about increasing political awareness among low-income Canadians?

Chapter 5: How Much Do Canadians Participate in Politics?

1 Why does it matter if many citizens choose not to vote?

2 Why do you think that turnout to vote is typically higher (or lower) in elections in your province or territory than it is in federal elections?

3 How would you account for the trend in turnout in elections in your province or territory?

4 Why are so many young Canadians not participating in politics?

5 Which is a more effective way of working for change, in your opinion: joining a political party or joining an interest group?

6 Should signing a petition or joining in a boycott of a product be considered a political act?

Chapter 6: How Civic-Minded Are Canadians?

1 Why do you think that Canada has a relatively high level of involvement in voluntary associations, compared with other established Western democracies?

2 Do you think that associational involvement is necessarily good for democracy?

3 How might the type of voluntary association to which people belong affect the amount of social capital that they are able to accumulate?

4 Why do you think that Canadians are volunteering fewer hours than they were in 1987?

5 How would you explain the link between philanthropy, volunteering, and political engagement?

Chapter 7: Engaging Canadians

1   Why do you think a university education enhances democratic citizenship?
2   Would providing more civics education in high school counteract the decline in political participation among young Canadians?
3   Should the media be encouraged to provide more coverage of political issues and policy debates?
4   How would you explain the provincial variations in democratic engagement?
5   Why do you think that the sense of civic duty to vote has declined?
6   If you had to recommend three steps that could be taken to enhance democratic citizenship in Canada, what would they be?

Additional Reading

Brenda O'Neill's "Generational patterns in the political opinions and behaviour of Canadians" (2001) provides an in-depth analysis of generational differences in political orientations and involvement in Canada. She examines whether today's young Canadians are more apathetic about politics and less engaged than previous generations were at the same age.

"Challenging the gendered vertical mosaic," by Yasmeen Abu-Laban (2002), provides a comprehensive survey of studies of the political participation of ethnic minorities in Canada, with particular attention to the intersection of ethnicity and gender. She argues that traditional conceptions of political participation need to be expanded in order to encompass the political activities of women and ethnic minorities.

In "Sugar and spice" (2002), Brenda O'Neill examines the nature and sources of "women's political culture" in Canada and how it affects women's political behaviour and political opinions. She pays particular attention to the relationship between women's socialization and their political values.

David Bedford and Sidney Pobihushchy's "On reserve status Indian voter participation in the Maritimes" (1995) analyzes voter turnout on reserves in New Brunswick, Nova Scotia, and Prince Edward Island, comparing turnout in federal and provincial elections with turnout in band elections. They argue that declining turnout in federal and provincial elections reflects a growing Aboriginal consciousness and a rejection of the Canadian electoral process as alien to traditional Aboriginal culture.

In *The decline of deference* (1996), Neil Nevitte links changes in Canadians' political orientations and behaviour to the larger process of value change that is under way in advanced industrial states and, in particular, to changing attitudes toward authority. The book makes extensive use of data on changing political, economic, and social values in the United States and Europe, as well as Canada.

Voter participation in Canada (2001), published by the Centre for Research and Information on Canada, provides a critical review of a variety of explanations that have been offered for the declining turnout to vote in Canada and proposes a number of possible ways to address the problem.

Patrick Fournier's "The uninformed Canadian voter" (2002) offers an assessment of how much Canadians know about politics, what determines their information level, and how their information level affects their political behaviour. *The challenge of direct democracy*, by Richard Johnston and his colleagues (1996), provides an extended assessment of low-information rationality arguments within the context of the vote in the 1992 referendum on the Charlottetown constitutional accord.

In "Civic literacy in comparative context" (2001), Henry Milner develops the concept of "civic literacy" to analyze the sources and implications of low levels of knowledge about politics. He also identifies policy initiatives that might be taken to increase the level of civic literacy in Canada. A much more extended treatment can be found in his recent monograph, *Civic literacy* (2002).

Paul Howe and David Northrup's "Strengthening Canadian democracy" (2000) provides a portrait of democratic malaise in Canada, based on a recent survey of Canadians' attitudes toward the basic structures of democratic government in Canada. The authors make extensive comparisons with the earlier findings of *Making representative democracy work* (1991), by André Blais and Elisabeth Gidengil.

In "Civic engagement, trust, and democracy" (2002), Lisa Young uses data from the 1999 Alberta Civil Society Survey to examine the argument that dissatisfaction with the quality of democratic life in Canada is linked to a decline in social capital. She finds evidence of an association between civic engagement, interpersonal trust, and confidence in government.

Caring Canadians, involved Canadians, by Michael Hall, Larry McKeown, and Karen Roberts (2001), provides a detailed analysis of findings from the 2000 National Survey on Giving, Volunteering and Participating, including comparisons with the results of a similar survey conducted in 1997.

"Referendums and initiatives: The politics of direct democracy," by Lawrence LeDuc (2002), examines the growing appeal of direct democracy and identifies the similarities and differences between referendums and elections. *Introducing direct democracy in Canada,* by Matthew Mendelsohn and Andrew Parkin (2001), assesses the merits and pitfalls of direct democracy to determine which types of direct democracy are most compatible with the values and traditions of Canadian democracy.

Works Cited

Abu-Laban, Yasmeen. 2002. Challenging the gendered vertical mosaic: Immigrants, ethnic minorities, gender, and political participation. In *Citizen politics: Research and theory in Canadian political behaviour,* ed. Joanna Everitt and Brenda O'Neill, 268-82. Don Mills, ON: Oxford University Press.

Althaus, Scott L. 1998. Information effects in collective preferences. *American Political Science Review* 92: 545-58.

Angell, Harold M. 1987. Duverger, Epstein and the problem of the mass party: The case of the Parti Québécois. *Canadian Journal of Political Science* 20: 363-78.

Ansalobehere, Stephen, Roy Behr, and Shanto Iyengar. 1993. *The media game.* New York: Macmillan.

Applied Research Branch. 2000. *Dropping out of high school: Definitions and costs.* R-01-1E. Ottawa: Human Resources Development Canada.

Barber, Benjamin R. 1984. *Strong democracy: Participatory politics for a new age.* Berkeley: University of California Press.

—. 1992. *An aristocracy of everyone.* New York: Ballantine Books.

Barney, Darin. Forthcoming 2005. *Communications Technology.* Canadian Democratic Audit. Vancouver: UBC Press.

Bartels, Larry M. 1996. Uninformed votes: Information effects in presidential elections. *American Journal of Political Science* 40:194-230.

Baum, Matthew A. 2002. Sex, lies, and war: How soft news brings foreign policy to the inattentive public. *American Political Science Review* 96: 91-109.

Bedford, David. 2003. Aboriginal voter participation in Nova Scotia and New Brunswick. *Electoral Insight* 5(3): 16-20.

Bedford, David, and Sidney Pobihushchy. 1995. On reserve status Indian voter participation in the Maritimes. *Canadian Journal of Native Studies* 15: 255-78.

Black, Jerome H. 1982. Immigrant political adaptation in Canada: Some tentative findings. *Canadian Journal of Political Science* 15: 9-27.

—. 1987. The practice of politics in two settings: Political transferability among recent immigrants to Canada. *Canadian Journal of Political Science* 20: 731-53.

—. 1991. Reforming the context of the voting process in Canada: Lessons from other democracies. In *Voter Turnout in Canada,* ed. Herman Bakvis. Vol. 15 of *Research studies of the Royal Commission on Electoral Reform and Party Financing.* Ottawa and Toronto: RCERPF/Dundurn Press.

—. 2000. The National Register of Electors: Raising questions about the new approach to voter registration in Canada. *Policy Matters* 1(10).

—. 2002. An update on ethnoracial minorities in the House of Commons. *Canadian Parliamentary Review* 25: 24-8.

Blais, André. 2000. *To vote or not to vote: The merits and limits of rational choice theory.* Pittsburgh: University of Pittsburgh Press.

Blais, André, and Agnieszka Dobrzynska. 1998. Turnout in electoral democracies. *European Journal of Political Research* 33: 239-61.

Blais, André, and Elisabeth Gidengil. 1991. *Making representative democracy work: The views of Canadians.* Vol. 17 of *Research studies of the Royal Commission on Electoral Reform and Party Financing (RCERPF).* Ottawa and Toronto: Dundurn Press.

Blais, André, Elisabeth Gidengil, Richard Nadeau, and Neil Nevitte. Forthcoming. The evolving nature of non-voting: Evidence from Canada. *European Journal of Political Research* 43: 221-36.

—. 2002. *Anatomy of a Liberal victory: Making sense of the 2000 Canadian election.* Peterborough, ON: Broadview Press.

Blais, André, Richard Johnston, Elisabeth Gidengil, and Neil Nevitte. 1996. La dynamique référendaire: Pourquoi les Canadiens ont-ils rejeté l'accord de Charlottetown? *Revue Française de Science Politique* 46: 817-30.

Butler, David, and Dennis Kavanagh. 1997. *The British general election of 1997.* London: Macmillan Press.

Cairns, Alan C. 2003. Aboriginal people's electoral participation in the Canadian community. *Electoral Insight* 5(3): 2-9.

Canadian Centre for Justice Statistics. 1997. *Canadian Crime Statistics, 1997.* Statistics Canada catalogue no. 85-002-XPE, vol. 18, no. 11. Ottawa, ON.

Canadian Election Study. 1997 and 2000. <www.fas.umontreal.ca/pol/ces-eec/index.html>. 6 February 2004.

—. 1965-1993. Inter-university Consortium for Political and Social Research. <www.icpsr.umich.edu>. 6 February 2004.

Canadian Opinion Research Archive. Queen's University, Kingston, ON. <www.queensu.ca/cora>. 6 February 2004.

Cappella, Joseph N., and Kathleen Hall Jamieson. 1997. *Spiral of cynicism: The press and the public good.* Oxford: Oxford University Press.

Centre for Research and Information on Canada (CRIC). 2001. *Voter participation in Canada: Is Canadian democracy in crisis?* CRIC Papers No. 3. Ottawa, ON.

Chui, Tina W.L., James E. Curtis, and Ronald D. Lambert. 1991. Immigrant background and political participation: Examining generational patterns. *Canadian Journal of Sociology* 16: 375-96.

Citizenship and Immigration Canada. 2002. *A Look at Canada.* Updated September 2002. <www.cic.gc.ca/english/citizen/look/look-ae.html>. 8 February 2004.

Clark, T.N., and M. Rempel. 1997. *Citizen politics in post-industrial societies.* Boulder, CO: Westview Press.

Clarke, Harold D., Jane Jenson, Lawrence LeDuc, and Jon H. Pammett. 1991. *Absent mandate: Interpreting change in Canadian elections.* 2nd ed. Toronto: Gage.

Clarkson, Stephen. 2001. The Liberal threepeat: The multi-system party in the multi-party system. In *The Canadian general election of 2000,* ed. Jon H. Pammett and Christopher Dornan, 13-57. Toronto: Dundurn Press.

Clement, Wallace. 1978. A political economy of regionalism. In *Modernization and the Canadian state,* ed. Daniel Glenday, Herbert Guindon, and Allan Turowetz, 89-110. Toronto: Macmillan.

Coleman, James S. 1988. Social capital in the creation of human capital. *American Journal of Sociology* 94: S95-120.

COMPAS Inc. 2001. I am Canadian? Canada Day poll. A COMPAS report to Global TV and *Ottawa Citizen,* Toronto and Ottawa. 21 June 2001. <www.compas.ca/pages/FrameMain.html>. 8 February 2004.

Converse, Philip E. 1990. Popular representation and the distribution of information. In *Information and democratic processes,* ed. John A. Ferejohn and James H. Kuklinski, 369-88. Chicago: University of Illinois Press.

—. 2000. Assessing the capacity of mass electorates. *Annual Review of Political Science* 3: 331-53.

Coupland, Douglas. 1991. *Generation X: Tales for an accelerated culture.* New York: St. Martin's Press.

Courtney, John C. 2004. *Elections.* Canadian Democratic Audit. Vancouver: UBC Press.

CRIC Trade Liberalization and Globalization Survey 2001. [0103]. Centre for Research and Information on Canada (CRIC), Ottawa, ON, Canadian Opinion Research Archive, Queen's University, Kingston, ON.

CROP sondage sur les élections québécoises 1989-1 (September 1989). [CR8909A]. CROP Inc., Montreal, QC, Canadian Opinion Research Archive, Queen's University, Kingston, ON.

CROP sondage auprès des Montréalais sur l'administration centrale (October 1990). [CR9010]. CROP Inc., Montreal, QC, Canadian Opinion Research Archive, Queen's University, Kingston, ON.

CROP les opinions et attitudes des résidents de la région de Montréal sur les questions scolaires (November 1990). [CR9011B]. CROP Inc., Montreal, QC, Canadian Opinion Research Archive, Queen's University, Kingston, ON.

Cross, William. 2004. *Political parties.* Canadian Democratic Audit. Vancouver: UBC Press.

Cutler, Fred. 2002. The simplest shortcut of all: Socio-demographic characteristics and electoral choice. *Journal of Politics* 64: 466-90.

Dahl, Robert A. 1967. The city in the future of democracy. *American Political Science Review* 61: 953-70.

Dalton, Russell. 1984. Cognitive mobilization and partisan dealignment in advanced industrial democracies. *Journal of Politics* 46: 264-84.

—. 2002. *Citizen politics: Public opinion and political parties in advanced industrial democracies.* 3rd ed. New York: Chatham House.

Dalton, Russell J., Ian McAllister, and Martin P. Wattenberg. 2000. The consequences of partisan dealignment. In *Parties without partisans: Political change in advanced industrial democracies,* ed. Russell J. Dalton and Martin P. Wattenberg, 37-63. New York: Oxford University Press.

Dalton, Russell J., and Martin P. Wattenberg, eds. 2002. *Parties without partisans: Political change in advanced industrial democracies.* New York: Oxford University Press.

Delli Carpini, Michael X., and Scott Keeter. 1996. *What Americans know about politics and why it matters.* New Haven, CT: Yale University Press.

Dewey, John. 1916. *Education and democracy.* New York: Macmillan.

—. 1938. *Experience and education.* London: Collier Macmillan.

Docherty. 2004. *Legislatures.* Canadian Democratic Audit. Vancouver: UBC Press.

Donohue, George A., Phillip J. Tichenor, and Clarice N. Olien. 1973. Mass media functions, knowledge and social control. *Journalism Quarterly* 50: 652-9.

Environment Canada. 1999. Urban air quality. *National Environmental Indicator Series.* Ottawa: Environment Canada.

Evans, Judith. 1980. Women and politics: A re-appraisal. *Political Studies* 28: 210-21.

Eveland, William P., Jr., and Dietram A. Scheufele. 2000. Connecting news media use with gaps in knowledge and participation. *Political Communication* 17: 215-37.

Feigenbaum, Harvey B., Jeffrey Henig, and Chris Hamnett. 1998. *Shrinking the state: The political underpinnings of privatization.* New York: Cambridge University Press.

Fiorina, Morris P. 1993. Explorations of a political theory of party identification. In *Classics in voting behaviour,* ed. Richard G. Niemi and Herbert F. Weisberg, 247-63. Washington, DC: CQ Press.

Fournier, Patrick. 2002. The uninformed Canadian voter. In *Citizen politics: Research and theory in Canadian political behaviour,* ed. Joanna Everitt and Brenda O'Neill, 92-109. Don Mills, ON: Oxford University Press.

Galston, William A. 2001. Political knowledge, political engagement, and civic education. *Annual Review of Political Science* 4: 217-34.

Gaziano, Cecilie, and Emanuel Gaziano. 1996. Theories and methods in knowledge gap research since 1970. In *An integrated approach to communication theory and research,* ed. M.B. Salwen and D.W. Stacks, 127-43. Mahway, NJ: Lawrence Erlbaum Associates.

Gidengil, Elisabeth. 1989. Diversity within unity: On analyzing regional dependency. *Studies in Political Economy* 29: 91-112.

—. 2002. The class voting conundrum. In *Political sociology: Canadian perspectives,* ed. Douglas Baer, 274-87. Don Mills: Oxford University Press.

Gidengil, Elisabeth, André Blais, Richard Nadeau, and Neil Nevitte. 2004. Language and cultural insecurity. In *Quebec: State and society,* ed. Alain Gagnon. 3rd ed. Peterborough, ON: Broadview Press.

Gidengil, Elisabeth, and Joanna Everitt. 1999. Metaphors and misrepresentation: Gendered mediation in news coverage of the 1993 Canadian leaders' debates. *Harvard International Journal of Press/Politics* 4: 48-65.

—. 2002. Damned if you do, damned if you don't: Television news coverage of female party leaders in the 1993 federal election. In *Political parties, representation and electoral democracy in Canada,* ed. William Cross, 223-37. Don Mills, ON: Oxford University Press.

—. 2003. Conventional coverage/unconventional politicians: Gender and media coverage of recent Canadian leaders' debates. *Canadian Journal of Political Science* 36: 559-77.

Goot, Murray, and Elizabeth Reid. 1975. *Women and voting studies: Mindless matrons or sexist scientism?* Sage Professional Papers in Contemporary Political Sociology. Beverly Hills, CA: Sage Publications.

Guérin, Daniel. 2003. Aboriginal participation in Canadian federal elections: Trends and implications. *Electoral Insight* 5(3): 10-15.

Hall, Michael, Larry McKeown, and Karen Roberts. 2001. *Caring Canadians, involved Canadians: Highlights from the 2000 National Survey of Giving, Volunteering and Participating.* Catalogue no. 71-542-XIE. Ottawa: Statistics Canada.

Hepburn, Mary A., Richard G. Niemi, and Chris Chapman. 2000. Service learning in college political science: Queries and commentary. *PS: Political Science* 33: 617-22.

Hibbing, John R., and Elizabeth Theiss-Morse. 1995. *Congress as public enemy: Public attitudes toward American political institutions.* Cambridge: Cambridge University Press.

Howe, Paul, and David Northrup. 2000. Strengthening Canadian democracy: The views of Canadians. *Policy Matters* 1(5).

Hunter, Anna. 2003. Exploring the issues of Aboriginal representation in federal elections. *Electoral Insight* 5(3): 27-33.

Hyman, Herbert, and Charles R. Wright. 1979. *Education's lasting influence on values.* Chicago: University of Chicago Press.

Indian and Northern Affairs Canada. 2000. *Comparison of social conditions, 1991 and 1996: Registered Indians, registered Indians living on reserve and the total population of Canada.* Ottawa: Minister of Indian Affairs and Northern Development.

Inglehart, Ronald. 1971. The silent revolution in Europe: intergenerational change in post-industrial societies. *American Political Science Review* 65: 991-1017.

—. 1990. *Culture shift in advanced industrial society.* Princeton, NJ: Princeton University Press.

Jenson, Jane. 1976. Party strategy and party identification. *Canadian Journal of Political Science* 9: 27-48.

Johnston, Richard, André Blais, Henry E. Brady, and Jean Crête. 1992. *Letting the people decide: Dynamics of a Canadian election.* Montreal: McGill-Queen's University Press.

Johnston, Richard, André Blais, Elisabeth Gidengil, and Neil Nevitte. 1996. *The challenge of direct democracy: The 1992 Canadian referendum.* Montreal: McGill-Queen's University Press.

Joslyn, Richard. 1984. *Mass media and elections.* New York: Random House.

Keeter, Scott. 1996. Origins of the disjunction of perception and reality: The cases of racial equality and environmental protection. Paper presented at the annual meeting of the American Political Science Association, San Francisco, 28 August-1 September.

Key, Vladimir O. 1966. *The responsible electorate: Rationality in presidential voting 1936-1960.* Cambridge, MA: Belknap Press of Harvard University Press.

Kinnear, Michael. 2003. The effect of expansion of the franchise on turnout. *Electoral Insight* 5(3): 46-50.

Kuklinski, James H., and Norman L. Hurley. 1994. On hearing and interpreting political messages: A cautionary tale of citizen cue-taking. *Journal of Politics* 56: 729-51.

Kuklinski, James H., and Paul J. Quirk. 2000. Reconsidering the rational public: Cognition, heuristics, and mass opinion. In *Elements of reason: Cognition, choice, and the bounds of rationality,* ed. Arthur Lupia, Matthew D. McCubbins, and Samuel L. Popkin, 153-82. Cambridge: Cambridge University Press.

Kuklinski, James H., Paul J. Quirk, Jennifer Jerit, David Schweider, and Robert F. Rich. 2000. Misinformation and the currency of democratic citizenship. *Journal of Politics* 62: 790-816.

Kushner, Joseph, David Siegel, and Hannah Stanwick. 1997. Ontario municipal elections: Voting trends and determinants of electoral success in a Canadian province. *Canadian Journal of Political Science* 30: 539-59.

Kwak, Nojin. 1999. Revisiting the knowledge gap hypothesis: Education, motivation, and media use. *Communication Research* 26: 385-413.

Ladner, Kiera L. 2003. The alienation of nation: Understanding Aboriginal electoral participation. *Electoral Insight* 5(3): 21-6.

Lambert, Ronald D., James E. Curtis, Steven D. Brown, and Barry J. Kay. 1986. In search of left/right beliefs in the Canadian electorate. *Canadian Journal of Political Science* 19: 541-63.

Lambert, Ronald D., James E. Curtis, Barry J. Kay, and Steven D. Brown. 1988. The social sources of political knowledge. *Canadian Journal of Political Science* 21: 359-74.

Lasswell, Harold. 1936. *Politics: Who gets what, when, how.* New York: P. Smith.

Lazarsfeld, Paul F., Bernard Berelson, and Hazel Gaudet. 1948. *The people's choice: How a voter makes up his mind in a presidential campaign.* New York: Columbia University Press.

LeDuc, Lawrence. 2002. Referendums and initiatives: The politics of direct democracy. In *Comparing democracies: New challenges in the study of elections and voting,* ed. Lawrence LeDuc, Richard Niemi, and Pippa Norris, 70-87. London: Sage.

Levin, Ben. 2000. Democracy and schools: Educating for citizenship. *Education Canada* 40: 4-7.

Little, Bruce. 1997. Good news, bad news, job numbers fuel for politicians of any stripe. *Globe and Mail,* 10 May, A1, A9.

Lupia, Arthur. 1994. Shortcuts versus encyclopedias: Information and voting behavior in California insurance reform elections. *American Political Science Review* 88: 63-76.

McDermott, Monika L. 1997. Voting cues in low-information elections: Candidate gender as a social information variable in contemporary United States elections. *American Journal of Political Science* 41: 270-83.

—. 1998. Race and gender cues in low-information elections. *Political Research Quarterly* 51: 895-918.

Mansbridge, Jane. 1980. *Beyond adversary democracy.* New York: Basic Books.

Mansbridge, Peter. 2002. Interview with Sarah Hampson. *Globe and Mail,* 22 June, R3.

Matthews, Ralph. 1983. *The creation of regional dependency.* Toronto: University of Toronto Press.

Mendelsohn, Matthew. 1993. Television's frames in the 1988 Canadian election. *Canadian Journal of Political Science* 18: 149-71.

—. 1996. Television news frames in the 1993 Canadian election. In *Seeing ourselves: Media power and policy in Canada,* ed. Helen Holmes and David Taras, 8-23. Toronto: Harcourt Brace.

Mendelsohn, Matthew, and Fred Cutler. 2000. The effect of referendums on democratic citizens: Information, politicization, efficacy and tolerance. *British Journal of Political Science* 30: 685-701.

Mendelsohn, Matthew, and Richard Nadeau. 1999. The rise and fall of candidates in Canadian election campaigns. *Harvard International Journal of Press/Politics* 4(2): 63-76.

Mendelsohn, Matthew, and Andrew Parkin. 2001. Introducing direct democracy in Canada. *Choices* 7(5).

Milner, Henry. 2001. Civic literacy in comparative context: Why Canadians should be concerned. *Policy Matters* 2(2).

—. 2002. *Civic literacy: How informed citizens make democracy work.* Hanover, NH: University Press of New England.

Moore, David W. 1987. Political campaigns and the knowledge-gap hypothesis. *Public Opinion Quarterly* 51: 186-200.

Morissette, René, Xuelin Zhang, and Marie Drolet. 2002. The evolution of wealth inequality. In *Canada, 1984-1999. No. 187.* Analytical Studies Branch research paper series. Ottawa: Statistics Canada.

Morland, Robert L. 1984. Municipal vs. national election voter turnout: Europe and the United States. *Political Science Quarterly* 99: 462-5.

Mutz, Diana C. 2002. The consequences of cross-cutting networks for political participation. *American Journal of Political Science* 46: 838-55.

Myers, John. 2000. Ontario's new civics course: Where's it going? Paper presented at the conference Citizenship 2000: Assuming Responsibility for Our Future, McGill Institute for the Study of Canada, Montreal, 20-1 October. <www.misc-iecm.mcgill.ca/citizen/myers2.htm>. 8 February 2004.

Nadeau, Richard, André Blais, Neil Nevitte, and Elisabeth Gidengil. 2000. It's unemployment, stupid! Why perceptions about the job situation hurt the Liberals in the 1997 election. *Canadian Public Policy* 26: 77-92.

Nadeau, Richard, and Thierry Giasson. 2003. Canada's democratic malaise: Are the media to blame? *Choices: Strengthening Canadian democracy,* vol. 9. Montreal: Institute for Research on Public Policy.

Nadeau, Richard, Neil Nevitte, Elisabeth Gidengil, and André Blais. 2002a. Election campaigns as information campaigns: Who learns what and with what effect. <www.fas.umontreal.ca/pol/ces-eec/publications1997.html# InformationCampaigns>. 8 February 2004.

—. 2002b. General political information, issue-specific knowledge, and policy preferences. Unpublished manuscript.

Nadeau, Richard, and Richard Niemi. 1995. Educated guesses: Survey knowledge questions. *Public Opinion Quarterly* 59: 323-46.

Nadeau, Richard, Richard Niemi, and Jeffrey Levine. 1993. Innumeracy about minority populations. *Public Opinion Quarterly* 57: 332-47.

Neuman, W. Russell. 1986. *The paradox of mass politics: Knowledge and opinion in the American electorate.* Cambridge, MA: Harvard University Press.

Nevitte, Neil. 1996. *The decline of deference.* Peterborough, ON: Broadview Press.

Nevitte, Neil, André Blais, Elisabeth Gidengil, and Richard Nadeau. 2000. *Unsteady state: The 1997 Canadian federal election.* Don Mills, ON: Oxford University Press.

Niemi, Richard G., Mary A. Hepburn, and Chris Chapman. 2000. Community service by high school students: A cure for civic ills? *Political Behavior* 22: 45-69.

Niemi, Richard G., and Jane Junn. 1998. *Civic education: What makes students learn.* New Haven, CT: Yale University Press.

Niemi, Richard G., and Julia Smith. 2001. Enrollments in high school government classes: Are we short-changing both citizenship and political science training? *PS: Political Science and Politics* 34(2): 281-7.

Norris, Pippa. 2001. *Digital divide? Civic engagement, information poverty and the Internet in democratic societies.* New York: Cambridge University Press.

—. 2002. *The democratic phoenix: Reinventing political activism.* New York: Cambridge University Press.

Norris, Pippa, John Curtice, David Sanders, Margaret Scammel, and Holli A. Semetko. 1999. *On message: Communicating the campaign.* London: Sage.

Oliver, J. Eric. 2000. City size and civic involvement in metropolitan America. *American Political Science Review* 94(2): 361-73.

O'Neill, Brenda. 2001. Generational patterns in the political opinions and behaviour of Canadians: Separating the wheat from the chaff. *Policy Matters* 2(5).

—. 2002. Sugar and spice? Political culture and the political behaviour of Canadian women. In *Citizen politics: Research and theory in Canadian political behaviour,* ed. Joanna Everitt and Brenda O'Neill, 40-55. Don Mills, ON: Oxford University Press.

Osborne, Ken. 1988. Political education for participant citizenship: Implications for the schools. In *Political education in Canada,* ed. Jon H. Pammett and Jean-Luc Pepin, 227-34. Halifax: Institute for Research on Public Policy.

—. 2000. Public schooling and citizenship education in Canada. *Canadian Ethnic Studies* 32: 8-37.

Page, Benjamin I. 1996. *Who deliberates? Mass media in modern democracy.* Chicago: University of Chicago Press.

Page, Benjamin I., and Robert Y. Shapiro. 1992. *The rational public: Fifty years of trends in Americans' policy preferences.* Chicago: University of Chicago Press.

Pintor, Rafael, and Maria Gratschew. 2002. *Voter turnout since 1945: A global report.* Stockholm: International Institute for Democracy and Electoral Assistance (IDEA). <www.idea.int/publications/turnout/VI_screenopt_2002.pdf>. 9 February 2004.

Plutzer, Eric. 2002. Becoming a habitual voter: Inertia, resources, and growth in young adulthood. *American Political Science Review* 96: 41-56.

Popkin, Samuel L. 1991. *The reasoning voter: Communication and persuasion in presidential campaigns.* Chicago: University of Chicago Press.

Popkin, Samuel L., and Michael A. Dimock. 1999. Political knowledge and citizen competence. In *Citizen competence and democratic institutions,* ed. Stephen L. Elkin and Karol Edward Soltan, 117-46. University Park: Pennsylvania State University Press.

Price, Vincent, and Mei-Ling Hsu. 1992. Public opinion about AIDS policies: The role of misinformation and attitudes towards homosexuals. *Public Opinion Quarterly* 56: 29-52.

Price, Vincent, and John Zaller. 1993. Who gets the news? Alternative measures of news perceptions and their implications for research. *Public Opinion Quarterly* 57: 133-64.

Putnam, Robert. 2000. *Bowling alone: The collapse and revival of American community.* New York: Simon and Schuster.

Rakow, Lana F., and Kimberlie Kranich. 1991. Women as sign in television news. *Journal of Communication* 41: 8-23.

Reed, Paul B., and L. Kevin Selbee. 2000. *Volunteering in Canada in the 1990s: Change and stasis.* Research report for the Nonprofit Sector Knowledge Base Project. Ottawa: Statistics Canada.

Rhee, J.W., and J.N. Cappella. 1997. The role of political sophistication in learning from news: Measuring schema development. *Communication Research* 24: 197-233.

Rosenstone, Steven, and John Hansen. 1993. *Mobilization, participation and democracy in America.* New York: Macmillan.

Royal Commission on Electoral Reform and Party Financing. 1991. *Reforming electoral democracy.* Vol. 1.

Sampert, Shannon, and Linda Trimble. 2003. Wham, bam, no thank you ma'am: Gender and the game frame in national newspaper coverage of election 2000. In *Women and electoral representation in Canada,* ed. Manon Tremblay and Linda Trimble, 211-27. Don Mills, ON: Oxford University Press.

Schattschneider, Elmer E. 1942. *Party government.* New York: Holt, Rinehart and Winston.

—. 1960. *The semisovereign people: A realist's view of democracy in America.* New York: Holt, Rinehart and Winston.

Sears, Alan, and Mark Perry. 2000. Paying attention to the contexts of citizenship education. *Education Canada* 40: 28-31.

Selznick, Gertrude, and Stephen Steinberg. 1969. *The tenacity of prejudice.* New York: Harper and Row.

Smiley, Marion. 1999. Democratic citizenship: A question of competence? In *Citizen competence and democratic institutions,* ed. Stephen L. Elkin and Karol Edward Soltan, 371-83. University Park: Pennsylvania State University Press.

Sniderman, Paul M., Richard A. Brody, and Philip E. Tetlock. 1991. *Reasoning and choice: Explorations in social psychology.* Cambridge: Cambridge University Press.

Sniderman, Paul M., Joseph F. Fletcher, Peter H. Russell, and Philip E. Tetlock. 1996. *The clash of rights: Liberty, equality, and legitimacy in pluralist democracy.* New Haven, CT: Yale University Press.

Statistics Canada. 1997 and 2000. National Survey of Giving, Volunteering and Participating. Survey number 4430. <www.statcan.ca/English/sdds/index.htm>. 9 February 2004.

—. 2002. Household Internet use survey. *The Daily,* 25 July. Updated 31 October 2002. <www.statcan.ca/Daily/English/020725/d020725a.htm>. 21 November 2003.

Stouffer, Samuel. 1955. Communism, conformity and civil liberties. New York: Doubleday.

Studlar, Donley T. 2001. Canadian exceptionalism: Explaining differences over time in provincial and federal voter turnout. *Canadian Journal of Political Science* 34: 299-319.

Tichenor, Phillip J., George A. Donohue, and Clarice N. Olien. 1970. Mass media flow and differential growth in knowledge. *Public Opinion Quarterly* 34: 159-70.

Ulbig, Stacy G., and Carolyn L. Funk. 1999. Conflict avoidance and political participation. *Political Behavior* 21: 265-82.

Van Aelst, Peter, and Stefaan Walgrave. 2001. Who is that (wo)man in the street? From the normalization of protest to the normalization of the protester. *European Journal of Political Research* 39: 461-86.

Verba, Sidney, Nancy Burns, and Kay Lehman Schlozman. 1997. Knowing and caring about politics: Gender and political engagement. *Journal of Politics* 59: 1051-72.

Verba, Sidney, and Norman H. Nie. 1972. *Participation in America: Political democracy and social inequality.* New York: Harper and Row.

Viswanath, Kasisomayajula, and John R. Finnegan Jr. 1996. The knowledge gap hypothesis: Twenty-five years later. In *Communication yearbook 19,* ed. B.R. Burleson, 187-227. Thousand Oaks, CA: Sage.

World Values Survey. Various years. <www.worldvaluessurvey.org>. 8 February 2004.

Young, Lisa. 2002. Civic engagement, trust, and democracy: Evidence from Alberta. In *Value change and governance in Canada,* ed. Neil Nevitte, 107-47. Toronto: University of Toronto Press.

Young, Lisa, and Joanna Everitt. 2004. *Advocacy groups.* Canadian Democratic Audit. Vancouver: UBC Press.

Young, Robert, Philippe Faucher, and André Blais. 1984. The concept of province-building: A critique. *Canadian Journal of Political Science* 17: 783-819.

Zaller, John. 1999. A theory of media politics: How the interests of politicians, journalists, and citizens shape the news. Unpublished typescript, UCLA. <www.uky.edu/AS/PoliSci/Peffley/pdf/ZallerTheoryofMediaPolitics(10-99). pdf>. 9 February 2004.

Index

A master index to all volumes in the Canadian Democratic Audit series can be found at www.ubcpress.ca/readingroom/audit/index.